Making Change

Making Change

The Decimalisation of Britain's Currency

Tom Hockenhull

The British Museum

SPINK

In memory of Mike Smith, who was working at
Birkenhead tax office on D-Day. To be honest,
he said, nothing much happened.

Published by Spink Books in collaboration with the British Museum
Text © 2021 The Trustees of the British Museum
Images © 2021 The Trustees of the British Museum,
unless otherwise indicated on page 80
Copyright © 2021 The Trustees of the British Museum

The moral right of Tom Hockenhull to be identified as the author of this
work has been asserted by him in accordance with the Copyright,
Designs and Patents Act of 1988.

All rights reserved. No part of this publication may be reproduced, stored in a
retrieval system or transmitted in any form or by any means, electronic, mechanical,
photocopying, recording or otherwise, without the prior permission of both the
copyright owner and the above publisher of this book.

A CIP catalogue record for this book is available from the British Library.

ISBN 978-1-912667-57-4

Design by Bobby Birchall, Bobby&Co.
Printed and bound by Gutenberg Press Ltd, Malta

Spink and Son Ltd, 69 Southampton Row, London WC1B 4ET

www.spinkbooks.com

Contents

Preface	6
The pound: the first 1,500 years	8
'What ought we to be doing about decimal coinage?'	15
Secret preparations	20
The competition	32
Exile from Tower Hill	48
The Decimal Currency Board	51
S.O.S.	59
A national effort	62
D-Day	68
Aftermath	75
Endnotes	78
Select bibliography	79
Acknowledgements	80
Picture credits	80

Preface

D-Day is Monday, 15th February 1971. On that day Decimal Currency starts, but it may be up to eighteen months before the 1d., 3d. and 6d. are demonetised. The ½d. is already demonetised and the 2/6 was demonetised in January 1970. The 1/- and 2/- pieces will continue to be legal tender equal to 5p and 10p respectively. This is the biggest financial change in our history.

From *Decimal Currency for Retailers in Tobacco*, 1970.

On 15 February 1971, 'D-Day', the UK overhauled its currency, simplifying its structure by reducing the number of pennies in the pound from 240 to an even 100, and abolishing all other subsidiaries. Decimalisation was the biggest single adjustment to the currency in its history, resulting in the retirement of the shilling, florin, half-crown and other popular coins. Just as significantly it required the breaking of a bond between the penny and the pound that had lasted more than a thousand years. Their relative values had never been altered, a longevity that remains unique among world currencies.

Successive governments and policymakers prided themselves on their ability to manage the value and global prestige of sterling. It had become constant and unchanging, the embodiment of its Middle English root, *ster*, meaning 'strength' or 'stability'. To ensure that decimalisation would not wreck public trust in the currency required careful coordination between the UK government, its appointed overseer the Decimal Currency Board (DCB) and the Royal Mint. Between them they worked to ensure public acceptance of the decimal system and its new coins. This is the story of how it happened.

Opposite: The UK pre-decimal penny, half-crown and shilling. Jack James, deputy master of the Royal Mint, lamented that British *£.s.d.* coins tended to get dirtier and more discoloured than coins of other countries owing to the intricacy of their designs.

The pound: the first 1,500 years

Probably the best way to get used to the new system will be to forget about the old as quickly as possible.

Which? magazine, November 1970.

The roots of pounds, shillings and pence lie in the sophisticated Roman currency system, imposed upon Britain by armies and administrators during the Roman conquest. Pound derives from *pondus*, the Latin word meaning weight. In the Roman world weight was measured in *libra* and *unciae*, from which we derive pounds (lbs) and ounces (oz) in the imperial weight system, as well as the present-day £ symbol, which is a barred 'L' for *librum* that came into use in the eighteenth century. Even under the Romans these measurements shifted to have a monetary function, with the gold solidus and silver denarius coins bearing a relationship to a libra weight. However, this system did not survive the collapse of Roman rule in Britain and, for almost 200 years from the early AD 400s to the 600s, the successor kingdoms we now commonly describe as Anglo-Saxon made no coins at all. When they did eventually revive the practice, they copied the coins being made by their nearest neighbours in modern France and western Germany. These small gold pieces were probably known as shillings, a word that meant 'fragment' or 'section', and they were relatively short-lived – the scarcity of gold led to their replacement with a silver equivalent between the AD 660s and 680s. Once again, these imitated developments in continental Europe and were the first local pennies, or *denarii*. In the eighth century King Offa of Mercia (reigned 757–96) changed the style of the penny to match the reforms of his Frankish contemporary, Charlemagne (reigned 768–814), and its value was now fixed at 240 per pound-weight of silver with an intermediate value of twelve pence, or a shilling. In England the main unit evolved to be called a pound, adopted from Germanic-speaking kingdoms, as in *pfund*, rather than a variation of the Latin *libra*, such as *livre* or *lira*, which became the standard unit in Romance language-speaking kingdoms. The word 'sterling' evolved later, around the twelfth century, and came to refer to the defined purity of the silver penny.

> *There are twenty shillings* [scillinga] *in a pound* [punde], *and twelve times twenty pence* [penega] *is a pound.*
> **From the *Enchiridion* [manual] by Byrhtferth, AD 1011.**

At first there were no coins issued above a silver penny in value. To the average person living in, for example, the eleventh century, who earned about a penny a day in wages (albeit with food, drink and lodging thrown in), the pound remained a theoretical value, rarely encountered except in accounting ledgers, mortgage agreements and other important financial documents. Furthermore, even in such documents one was almost as likely to encounter values measured in marks (80 silver pennies, or one-third of a pound), such was the interchangeability of such terms in the English currency.

The gradual expansion of the economy in the twelfth and thirteenth centuries necessitated the introduction of higher value coins – first a two-pence, then a silver shilling, and in the fourteenth century a gold coinage to supplement the silver. The first of these was called a florin, imitating the gold coins being issued by the wealthy Tuscan city of Florence, from which it took its name. In 1489 the first coin valued at a pound was issued, which was called a sovereign because it featured a full-length seated portrait of King Henry VII. However, this large gold coin was more of a prestige piece than a practical component of the currency and, owing to its enormous value, it appears to have been used only infrequently in transactions. In time it was revalued upwards to thirty shillings as the price of gold increased relative to silver, a reminder that the silver penny remained the standard unit against which the gold coinage was measured. Likewise, the seventeenth-century guinea was revalued from twenty shillings to twenty-one when its bullion value increased relative to silver. In the nineteenth century the pound became a gold standard currency, accompanied by the first regular issue of a pound coin, which took its name from Henry VII's sovereign, from 1817. The nineteenth-century sovereign, with its soon-to-become iconic design featuring St George and the dragon by Benedetto Pistrucci (1783–1855), became a mainstay of the currency, emblematic of Britain's rise as a global power. By the last years of Queen Victoria's reign, it was being minted across the British Empire.

A decimalised currency had been under discussion since at least the seventeenth century. Early advocates included the influential economist Sir William Petty (1623–87) who, in 1682, proposed a system to 'keep all Accompts in a way of Decimal Arithmetick'. His contemporary Sir Christopher Wren (1632–1723) argued that a forthcoming re-coinage, due in 1696, provided the ideal opportunity to introduce a decimal currency, since the old coins were to be recalled anyway. His lead unit was to be called the 'noble', it being a popular gold coin, divided into 10 primes and 100 seconds. However, the opportunity was not taken and in 1704 Russia grabbed the glory of being the first country to introduce a decimal currency under the reforms of Peter the Great (reigned 1682–1725). At the end of that century, in 1795, the French replaced their livre, which had become greatly devalued by the events of the Revolution, with a decimalised franc, part of a grand project to metricise everything including weights, measures, dates and even time. Snubbing the British system, the dollar currency of the newly independent United States of America was decimalised at the insistence of Thomas Jefferson (1743–1826), who had studied the French currency reforms. Yet more states followed suit – the Netherlands in 1817, Sweden in 1855, the Austro-Hungarian Empire in 1857, Japan in 1868 and the German Empire in 1873.

Above: George III gold sovereign, 1818.

British intransigence was in part down to a reticence among politicians to upset tradition: the longer a system remains unchanged, the more embedded it becomes in the cultural and economic fabric of a nation. During the nineteenth century there was also a hint of exceptionalism in the stubborn notion of 'going it alone'. To have followed victory against Napoleon's armies by adopting the same currency system as France would have seemed like a capitulation to the Establishment. Yet there was a growing perception that a decimal system would make the pound more compatible with other emerging global currencies, and thus more competitive. Mutterings in the press regarding the usefulness of a decimal system occasionally broke into the public discourse, especially during periods of relative peace and prosperity, and in 1841 a Decimalisation Association was founded to agitate for reform. Appeasing these interests, the introduction of a silver 2*s.* coin, a florin in 1849, created a decimal unit in the pounds, shillings and pence system (£.*s.d*), a 24*d.* coin worth one-tenth of a pound.

This low-key move precipitated a decade of debate and discussion regarding the merits of a decimal currency. In 1853, a Parliamentary Select Committee was appointed to investigate, but in 1854 William Gladstone (1809–98), then chancellor of the exchequer, summed up the prevailing mood in government when he said that:

Above: 1849 UK florin. The coin was nicknamed the 'godless' florin owing to the omission of *Dei Gratia*, 'By the Grace of God', from the legend.

> I cannot doubt that a decimal system would be of immense advantage in money transactions…[b]ut I do not think we have obtained sufficient evidence as to the sense and feeling of the country with respect to it. It is, as you are aware, the enormous masses of the community who have immense business to transact who must guide the Government in the matter.

Citing the 'established habits of the people' a Royal Commission of 1856–59 reported that decimalisation 'does not appear desirable, under existing circumstances'.

In 1865 France, Italy, Belgium and Switzerland established the Latin Monetary Union through which they agreed to issue a decimal gold standard coinage based on the French franc. At the International Monetary Conference convened in Paris in 1867, representatives from several nations were invited to discuss how this could be practically implemented. Rather out of politeness than genuine enthusiasm for the project, the British Government dispatched Charles Rivers Wilson (1831–1916) of the Treasury and Thomas Graham (1805–69), master of the Mint, with instructions merely to observe the proceedings. However, it hadn't reckoned on Graham emerging as an enthusiastic supporter of a decimalised international currency. In preparation for the conference he had the Mint produce two pattern-coins – a gold 100 pence/ducat and a silver 10 pence/franc. These he shared with the other delegates along with his proposal for a system based upon a 10-franc unit,

Above: Silver 1 franc/10 pence pattern-coin, 1867.

having calculated that this would have required just a 4 per cent reduction in the value of the penny to achieve decimalisation. He and Rivers Wilson proposed the same system in a subsequent report, upon receipt of which the Government felt obliged to investigate, and it duly convened a Royal Commission. This Commission, however, poured cold water on their proposal, not least because it would require the withdrawal of all the UK gold coinage.

Decimalisation dropped back down the agenda and wouldn't receive full reconsideration until after the First World War. Reporting in 1920, a Royal Commission repeated its findings from earlier Commissions. In reaching its conclusions it noted that the public response had been tepid, which is perhaps not surprising given its timing – a nation recovering from four years of devastation was unlikely to welcome yet more upheaval.

A lack of coherence among decimalisation's supporters on which system to adopt, and how the current system should be adapted, resulted in countless treatises arguing for one system over another. The causes of the disagreements were apparently limitless, from the name of the lead unit and its sub-denomination(s), to the number of factors. Should it be measured in factors of 10 (a decimal system), or a duodecimal system (factors of 12)? The factors of a decimal system are 1, 2 and 5, while a duodecimal system has a greater range of factors – 1, 2, 3, 4 and 6. John Maynard Keynes (1883–1946) said that 'I confess to some emotions of duo-decimal conservatism. I have always thought that the decimalisation which the Aryans brought in was a trifle vulgar and that the Sumerian origins of our civilisation were more distinguished when they duo-decimalised the fundamental concepts for measuring time and money which they invented.' With opinion divided even among advocates of currency reform, it is perhaps small wonder that the issue lay dormant. Even as late as 1955 an attempt to pass a decimal currency bill through Parliament fell at the second reading.

Then, just as it looked like the matter might be swept under the carpet for another generation, the government found itself under pressure from member states of the Commonwealth. An unintended consequence of the end of empire was that former British colonies were now modernising their currencies and, in doing so, rejecting the principles of £.s.d. In 1957 India decimalised the rupee from 16 anna and 64 paise to 100 naya paise, while in South Africa a

1958 report committed the country to putting the currency on a 10-shilling equivalent unit. There were similar commitments from New Zealand, Australia and the Republic of Ireland.[1] Australia had flirted with calling its new currency the 'royal' but opted instead for a more neutral term, the dollar, divided into cents. In South Africa the subsequent introduction of the rand (a new currency) in 1961 was a further demonstration of the hostile Afrikaner government's efforts to distance itself from the Commonwealth, which it left in the same year. The only non-decimal currencies left would soon be those of the UK, Nigeria, Malta and the Gambia. Within just a few years Britain's idiosyncratic £.s.d. system had become exposed and isolated on the world stage, and the government was forced to act.

Above: Australia's decimal 50-cent coin, first issued in 1966. This was the first coin series to feature the portrait of the Queen designed by Arnold Machin.

'What ought we to be doing about decimal coinage?'[2]

In 1960 the Conservative government appointed a joint committee to report on both a metric measurement system and a decimal currency. Headed by the British Association for the Advancement of Science and Association of British Chambers of Commerce, this report came out in favour of a decimal coinage and suggested that the time had come for a decision to be made. However, it noted, only the UK government could commit to such a decision. The government's initial response was non-committal, announcing that it would welcome a public discussion, which was another way of saying that it hoped the matter would just disappear. But then came

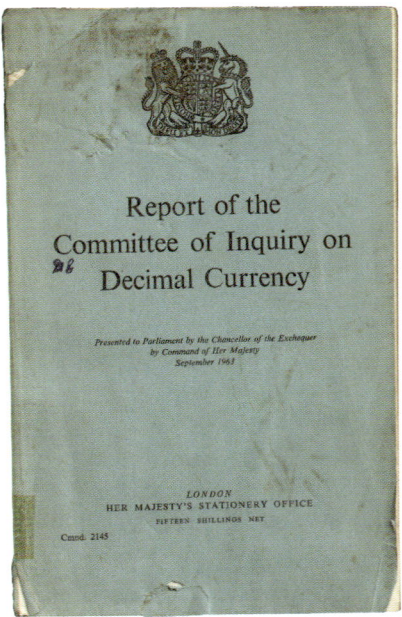

Left: A well-thumbed library copy of the Halsbury Report, published 1963.

the appointment of a new chancellor, Selwyn Lloyd (1904–78), in July 1960. More enthusiastic about decimalisation than his predecessor, Lloyd set up a working party comprising officials from the Treasury, Royal Mint, Board of Trade, Post Office and the Bank of England, all of whom came out in favour of decimalisation. This was followed by a Cabinet decision in November 1961 to appoint a Committee of Inquiry chaired by Tony Giffard, 3rd Lord Halsbury (1908–2000). The Halsbury Committee was tasked with advising on the most practical form the currency could take, the timing of its introduction and an estimate of the costs. The one question it wasn't required to answer was whether decimalisation should happen at all – this, it seems, had already been decided in principle. On the Committee were Dame Ann Godwin, chair of the TUC; Roy Allen, professor of statistics at London University; Ronald Thornton, vice chairman of Barclays Bank; Vernon Ely, owner of the department store Elys of Wimbledon and J.M.A. Smith, lately assistant managing director of Ford Motor Company. Its findings were published in September 1963.

The committee had discussed potential names for the currency, narrowing the list from twenty-five to four (including a florin-cent and a 5-shilling cent), and then two – a 10-shilling unit divided into 100 cents or a retained pound unit divided into 100 pennies. Four committee members favoured a currency based on the pound, while Ely and Smith signed a memorandum of dissent expressing preference for a 10-shilling system. Godwin, the TUC chair, and Allen, the statistics professor, had initially supported the 10-shilling system, but appear to have been won over to the pound/pence argument. It has been suggested that they were influenced by the warm and personable Halsbury. Although a scientist by training who took evidence seriously, he 'had a prejudice in favour of such amiable relics as the £ [pound] and the penny, and often proclaimed that "the name of the penny must never be lost!"'[3] Ely and Smith were, by contrast, less popular among the Committee's members and came across as bigoted and somewhat narrow-minded. Ely, who believed that the 10-shilling system worked in favour of retail interests, felt particularly strongly and was still haranguing the chancellor on the subject five years later.

There were yet more delays to come, caused by turmoil within Whitehall: Harold Macmillan (1894–1986) resigned as prime minister in October 1963 and was replaced by Sir Alec Douglas-Home (1903–95). In November 1963 Douglas-Home wrote to his chancellor,

Reginald Maudling, asking 'what ought we to be doing about decimal coinage? One is tempted to leave it alone: but I am afraid that mere postponement will get us the worst of all possible worlds', to which Maudling replied, 'I share your reluctance'. Both were perhaps recognising that an election was due within twelve months and the Tories were behind Labour in the polls. The motives behind an adjournment of UK decimalisation were now also practical, as the planned decimalisation of Australia and New Zealand's currencies, in 1966 and 1967 respectively, was drawing close. It was deemed advisable to wait for these countries to get the decimalisation of their currencies out of the way to relieve the burden on cash register and other coin-operated machine manufacturers. Australia in particular was a large export market for British machines and, if it went over to a decimal currency at the same time, the period required for UK changeover would have to be lengthened, significantly increasing the cost. This was already estimated at £100 million.

After the 1964 election, which was narrowly won by Labour, the decision fell to the new prime minister, Harold Wilson (1916–1995) and his chancellor, James Callaghan (1912–2005), who was an enthusiastic supporter of decimalisation. 'I very much regret that we're the last

Above: TUC chair Dame Ann Godwin and Lord Halsbury.

country to adopt it', he would later say. 'The cost of going decimal is heavy, but you recover it within a year or two and from then on you get a permanent bonus all the way through'. Yet he could do nothing while Labour had only a tiny majority and, besides, the Wilson government's priority throughout 1964–5 was the ultimately fruitless endeavour of defending the pound against foreign speculation. By early 1966 the easing of economic pressures and predictions of a large majority in the forthcoming election eased the prime minister's nerves, and in February 1966 Callaghan broached the issue once more. A twenty-second conversation ended with an almost casual 'why not?' from Wilson. On 1 March 1966 Callaghan announced to the House of Commons that the UK currency would be going decimal.

Both the chancellor and prime minister were determined that the major unit should be based on the pound, not a 10-shilling unit. Back in 1961 on the BBC's *Any Questions*, Wilson had said 'not only Britain and the sterling area, but the whole world will lose something if the pound disappears from the markets of the world.' Callaghan was perhaps the less determined of the two to have a currency based on the pound unit, though if any doubts lingered they were put to rest by a report from the Australian Treasury, which said it wished that it had followed the pound basis rather than the shilling when it implemented decimalisation, as the conversion of financial records had been a nightmare. In fact, the argument could have gone either way and there was no clear advantage or disadvantage to either system. What won over was perhaps the emotional argument that the pound was the bigger, more established unit of the two, the one that was already used for overseas transactions, albeit interchangeably with the name 'sterling'. It was also considered important to retain the immediately recognisable barred 'L' for *libra* pound symbol.

This was far from the end of the matter. The pound versus shilling debate flared up again following publication of the government White Paper on decimalisation in December 1966, in which the government set out its intention to have a pound-based major unit. Some concerns were well-founded – the chief anxiety was that prices would go up, especially of cheaper foodstuffs. This would be caused by the new smallest unit, the halfpenny, being worth 1.2*d*. in old money or 2.4*d*. if the halfpenny were to be abolished. Put another way, until the old ½*d*. was withdrawn in 1969, fractions of a pre-decimal pound could be as low as 1/480th, whereas after decimalisation this would be reduced to 1/200th. It was further argued that a 10-shilling system, with greater associability to £.s.d., would have made it harder for retailers to disguise price rises. The involvement of interest groups was extensive, but largely ineffectual. The Consumer Council set up a Decimal Action Committee arguing for a 10-shilling system in January 1967 but couldn't agree on what should be the smallest denomination, which undermined its effectiveness as a campaign.

There was also the question of what to call the decimal subunit. When other countries had decimalised, they had invariably called the new subunit a cent. However, Halsbury had expressed a preference for retaining the penny and Callaghan shared his opinion on this 'amiable relic': 'oh, I much prefer "penny"', he said, 'why should we go American – penny is good, it is indeed the oldest coin in Britain, it was originally a silver coin. I see no reason why we should adopt cent, it's a miserable sounding word by comparison with penny.'

Determined to press ahead and stick to a deadline of February 1971 as set out in the White Paper, Wilson imposed a two-line whip when the Decimal Currency Bill was read in Parliament in March 1967. It received its second reading with a majority of 261 to 169, passed its third reading and received Royal Assent on 13 July 1967. A second bill set out detailed arrangements for the changeover and provided for a transition period when both new and old coins would remain legal tender, and in which accounts could be written in either pre-decimal or decimal amounts. It received its second reading on the evening of 30 January 1969, the day in which the Beatles performed their rooftop concert up the road at Apple Corps, and passed into law in May of that year.

Secret preparations

The Royal Mint Advisory Committee (RMAC) sits within the Royal Mint. On the Committee are people knowledgeable in history and the arts who consult on matters concerning the design of seals, medals, coins and decorations. In the 1960s its twelve-strong panel of distinguished advisors included the poet (and founding member of the Victorian Society) John Betjeman (1906–84); Sir Robin Darwin (1910–74), rector of the Royal College of Art and the art historian Sir Kenneth Clark (1903–83). Its President was HRH Prince Philip, Duke of Edinburgh (b. 1921).

Following the government's appointment of the Halsbury Committee Sir Jack James (1906–1980), deputy master of the Royal Mint, wrote to members of the RMAC in early 1962 asking them to review the present coinage and to suggest how new decimal designs might be chosen. His aim was to prepare the Mint for any government announcement on decimalisation as a result of the impending report from the Halsbury Committee. The RMAC proposed that artists should be invited to compete in groups or teams, under the utmost secrecy, to come up with fresh sets of decimal designs for both the front and back of the coins. With new denominations to be introduced, a redesign of the reverses was essential. The front of the coins could, in theory, continue to use the 1953 coronation portrait by Mary Gillick (1881–1965) but this idea was quickly rejected as it would look outdated by the time the decimal coins were finally issued.

Various arts bodies including the Royal Academy (RA), Royal Institute of British Architects (RIBA), Faculty of Royal Designers for Industry (RDI) and the Royal College of Art (RCA) were approached. Between them they put forward a range of artistic talents from a variety of disciplines, young and old, both eminent and relatively unknown. From the RA its president, Sir Charles Wheeler (1892–1974), put forward only three names – himself, the Scottish sculptor William McMillan (1887–1977), who had previously been runner-up in a competition to design the coin portrait of Edward VIII, and a younger designer named Arnold Machin (1911–99). Wheeler clearly hoped that this small pool would increase his own chances of being selected. Meanwhile, RIBA submitted designs by just two entrants, one of whom was an architect and the other was the renowned war artist and illustrator Edward Bawden (1903–89). Finally, the RDI and RCA formed a joint third team bursting with creativity and energy, whose members included the modernist sculptor Geoffrey Clarke (1924–2014), Reynolds Stone (1909–79) and Christopher Ironside (1913–92).

The RCA/RDI team took to the task with enthusiasm, producing new designs and exploring the boundaries of what was technically achievable. Geoffrey Clarke's ideas were particularly experimental. He proposed dish-shaped coins and designs where all the textual information is restricted to one side. His effigy of the Queen is equally adventurous. Sunk into the surface, it eschews a representative design for a stylistic portrait reminiscent of British Iron-Age (pre-Roman) coins. One question raised by the team, possibly at Clarke's instigation, was whether lettering could be put on the outside edge of a coin in place of a grooved (milled) edge, a query that foreshadowed the 1983 £1 coin with its edge inscription *DECUS ET TUTAMEN* ('a decoration and a safeguard').

By December 1962, the RMAC had narrowed the list of potential candidates to Edward Bawden from the RIBA team, Christopher Ironside from the RCA/RDI team and Arnold Machin from the RA team. For the back of the coins, Machin's ideas were quickly rejected as unsuitable, which left the submissions from Ironside and Bawden to consider. Although the Committee liked Bawden's designs, it commented that they were somewhat flattered by his superior skill as

Above: Geoffrey Clarke's plaster models for the decimal coinage. The RMAC ultimately decided that Clarke's ideas were more radical than the brief required, and they were taken no further.

a draughtsman and might look bleak when made into coins. Overall, the RMAC concluded, Ironside's reverse ideas were more suited to coinage, and it was these that were progressed to the next stage.

For the portrait side, the shortlisted artists were required to create a plaster relief of the Queen from photographs taken by Antony Armstrong-Jones, Earl of Snowden (1930–2017). Based on these, the RMAC invited Ironside and Machin to develop their ideas, each submitting about a half-dozen models. At about this time Robin Darwin, who was Ironside's friend, boss at the RCA and champion on the Advisory Committee, leaked Machin's designs to him, suggesting that he copy them to gain the upper hand in the competition. Ironside firmly rejected the suggestion and, when he later told Machin what had happened, both laughed at Darwin's mendacity. Machin's designs did indeed emerge as the favourite, with John Betjeman declaring enthusiastically that he had 'made her look a bit sexy', and he was duly selected to produce the Queen's portrait for the coinage.

Although just a couple of years separated them in age, Christopher Ironside and Arnold Machin came from very different backgrounds. Born in 1913 into an upper middle-class family, Ironside had received a public school education at Bradfield College, in Berkshire, which he hated: 'the idea of razing the establishment to the ground and

Left: Christopher Ironside examines one of his plaster models for the decimal coinage, 1968. In the background a previous medal commission from the Royal Mint sits on the sideboard.

sowing the site with salt gave [me and my brother, Robin] pleasure and spiritual refreshment', he later said. His further studies included life drawing at London County Council Central School of Arts and Crafts, where he tried sculpture for the first time, 'supposedly to improve my drawing', he claimed. After spending the war at the Directorate of Camouflage (Ministry of Home Security) and then the Council of Industrial Design he became a part-time tutor in life drawing at the RCA from 1953. While there he took on numerous private commissions including theatre set designs, sculptures, exhibition installations, paintings and book illustrations. From the mid-1950s he began to design medals including the Benjamin Franklin award for the Royal Society of Arts in 1956 and Kenyon medal for the British Academy inaugurated in 1957. The promise he showed as a medals designer led to the invitation to join the RCA/RDI team.

Machin, by contrast, came from a modest background. Born in Stoke-on-Trent in 1911, he was apprenticed to Minton pottery at the age of fourteen to paint china and then studied sculpture at the local art college. He might have remained in the potteries all his life had it not been for the Great Depression and the ensuing slump of the 1930s, which caused him to try his luck with a move to Royal Crown Derby. While there he studied part-time at Derby College of Art before being awarded a scholarship to the Royal College of Art in 1937. Retaining his close links with the potteries, he fell under the patronage of Josiah Wedgwood and Sons Ltd, for whom he modelled numerous busts and portrait medallions. *Spring*, a life-size full-length figure with cherubs, was exhibited in the Royal Academy Summer Exhibition in 1947, the year he was elected an associate. By the early 1960s he was master of sculpture at the Royal Academy School, a position he held until 1967. Known as a quiet man albeit with strong principles, he was imprisoned as a conscientious objector for nine months during the Second World War. He became a minor celebrity when, in 1956, he chained himself to the Victorian gas lamp outside his home in Stoke, protesting its removal and replacement with a modern concrete post. The campaign was unsuccessful, but he was given the old post by the council, which he installed in his garden. Although he had produced portrait likenesses in relief during his time at Wedgwood, he had not designed a coin before the teams competition.

Machin was now required to produce a likeness of the Queen in clay based on four sittings in an upstairs room at Buckingham Palace.

The outcome wasn't entirely satisfactory so he asked for one final sitting, for which he had to journey to Balmoral Castle where the royals were spending the summer break. There he was given a tour of the estate and invited to a special dinner celebrating the announcement that the Queen was expecting a fourth child. Each sitting took about an hour, and Machin found the Queen to be a relaxed and genial host with a good sense of humour, arriving at one sitting with curlers still in her hair. On another occasion the Duke of Edinburgh came up to look at Machin's relief, declaring that 'it wants a bit more on the chin'. Machin duly added more clay only to take it off again (to the Queen's delight) when the Duke had left the room. Upon Machin's arrival back at home from Balmoral, the family received a parcel containing a brace of grouse, which they gave away because they were vegetarian.

In April 1964 the RMAC approved Machin's obverse design for the coinage. At the press launch the Mint took pains to point out that the new effigy was not linked to the rumoured UK decimal coinage, although the inference could scarcely be avoided. In fact, it would first appear on Australia's decimal coins in 1966. Machin was awarded an OBE in 1965 and in the following year he was commissioned to design the portrait of the Queen for use on the postage stamps, a design which the Queen resisted updating thereafter due to her satisfaction with the outcome. Today visitors to Newcastle-Under-Lyme can pay tribute to Machin with a visit to the local JD Wetherspoon pub, which is named in his honour.

Left: Machin's portrait of the Queen on the UK 10 new pence coin, 1968.

The development of the decimal reverses proved a great deal more tortuous, with numerous setbacks and uncertainties following Ironside's selection from the teams competition in 1963. Ironside commenced work on four sets of drawings combining various elements of heraldic imagery. The 50p from set 'A' features St George and the dragon, while the ½p includes the rose, thistle, leek and shamrock representing the four constituents of the United Kingdom. Heraldic shields are the focus of set 'B', the 1p featuring a shielded Union Jack, while set 'C' features royal symbolism such as a crown on the penny. A fourth set ditches the heraldic imagery in favour of less traditional designs – a sun on the 50p and a rope design on the penny, for example. These preliminary ideas were prepared as pencil sketches and then photographed and mounted on cardboard for consideration by the RMAC.

Ironside was invited to progress set 'C' to the next stage. The first version of these, completed at the end of 1963, includes designs for a farthing (1/4p), ½p, 1p and 20p, the last of which features the Royal Coat of Arms. Designs for a 2p and 10p, featuring Britannia and St George and the dragon respectively, took much longer to materialise.

For the 2p, Ironside experimented by overlapping the figure of Britannia with the denominations, remarking that if this were an option, then various new possibilities would open up, '[b]ut I would not recommend the pose in copper because it would cause confusion.'

Above: Arnold Machin with his portrait of the Queen used on the postage stamps.

26 Making Change

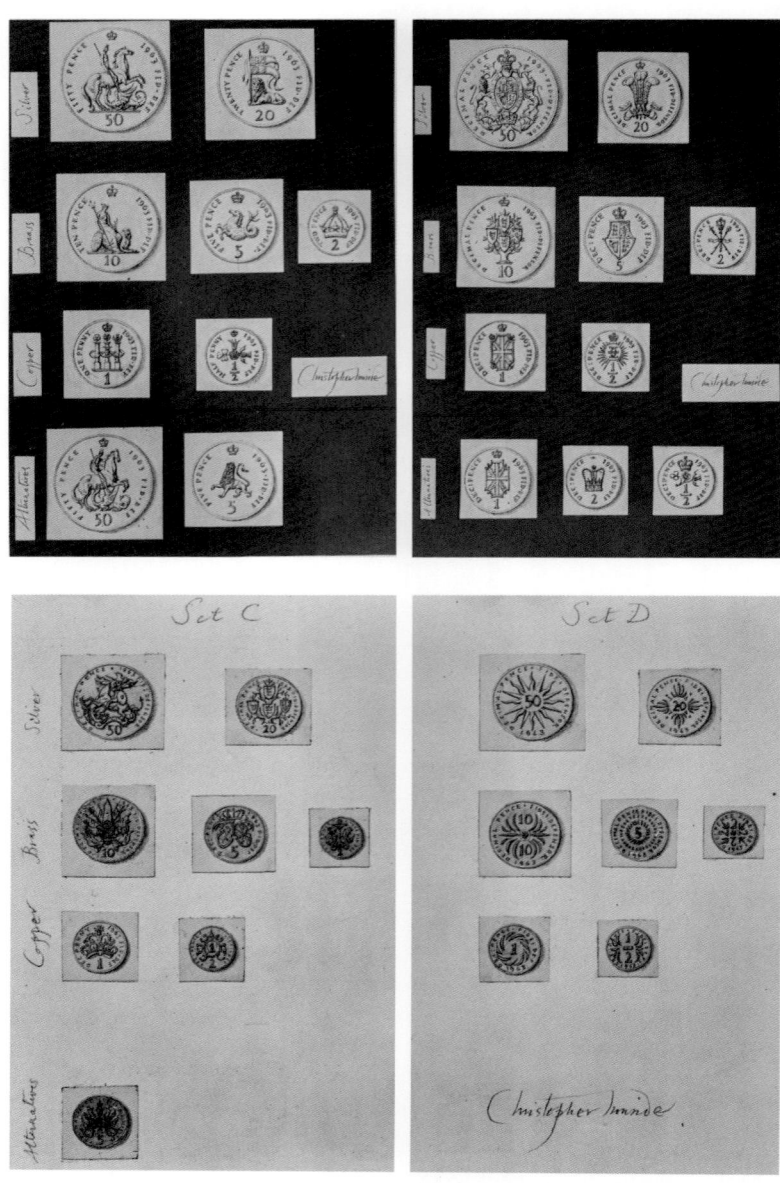

Above: Photographs of Ironside's 1963 designs comprising four sets, A, B, C and D.

Many versions followed and in frustration he wrote that 'when I get a pencil in my hand to design another Britannia I begin to feel foggy between the ears.' He elected to start afresh, coming up with an entirely new set of Britannia drawings and, by 1965, progress had been sufficient enough that he was asked to reproduce it in plaster. In March 1966 the RMAC approved this design, albeit with the proviso that Ironside rework the head and neck, as the plaster model had turned out chubbier than in his drawings.

Like most engravers, Ironside made his plaster models by tracing a drawing in reverse directly onto a blank plaster of Paris disc, about an inch thick and roughly the diameter of a small dinner plate, the surface of which was cast from plate glass so that it was free from blemishes.

Above: Ironside produced several variations on the same theme for his 10p design featuring St George and the dragon.

He then proceeded to carve into its soft surface, preferring to work in the negative, and thus in reverse. Another cast would be taken in the positive, with more detail added with each casting until he was satisfied. The Mint periodically dispatched a chauffeur-driven car to collect the finished plasters in little white boxes that, remarked his wife Jean, made them look like a pizza delivery. These were taken to the Mint and reproduced in metal via the electrotyping process. The electrotype was placed in a reducing machine, an eighteenth-century invention based on a pantograph that saved the eyesight of many an engraver. It works by 'reading' the contours of the electrotype using a fine needle and a system of pulleys that scales the design down to make a miniature copy, or reduction, from which the die is ultimately produced for striking the coins.

Above: Drawings for the 2p coin featuring Britannia by Christopher Ironside, 1963–4.

Development of the decimals took place in utmost secrecy. Working from his home in Kensington, Ironside was forbidden from talking to anyone about his work. Most instructions from the Mint were received by telephone, while the occasional letter was marked 'STRICTLY CONFIDENTIAL'. The secrecy, says Jean, 'made life rather difficult at home…[w]ith a teenage daughter at the top of the house, an elderly mother on the ground floor and two babies arriving in quick succession, there was little room at home for a discreet place to work.' On one occasion Ironside's young daughter climbed out of her cot and was discovered at his desk, happily digging his tools into a finished plaster. Ironside took to working at one end of the drawing room, throwing a cloth over his work any time that friends called by, while more plaster casts were stacked out of sight on a balcony.

Above: Plaster model for the 2p coin by Christopher Ironside, 1966.

His efforts at concealment failed one evening when two friends, who had been invited to dinner, took a stroll on the balcony while he was downstairs making coffee. '"You're designing the decimals!" they cried,' recalls Jean. '"You haven't seen a thing!" growled Christopher. "If you say anything, they will put me in the Tower!"'

The government's announcement on decimalisation in March 1966 caught the Mint somewhat by surprise, and a set of pattern coins with Ironside's designs was hastily produced. Besides Britannia and St George on the 2p and 10p these pattern coins feature the Welsh Dragon on the ½p, Scottish shields on the 1p, three crowns representing the Order of Bath on the 5p and, on the 20p, the Royal Coat of Arms.

In July 1966 the patterns were shown to cabinet ministers. The response was less than enthusiastic. Most vocal among their critics was Niall MacDermot (1916–96), financial secretary to the Treasury who wrote a lengthy dismissal, describing the designs as 'bad, fussy and "old hat"'. Ministers' overall response was more measured yet critical nevertheless, regarding the designs as too complicated and failing to adequately reflect parliamentary tradition. This was a blow to the RMAC, which had invested almost three years in developing Ironside's designs. Feeling that the role of the Committee had been undermined, the Duke of Edinburgh even briefly considered resigning. Instead, in August 1966, he wrote to the chancellor suggesting that, since ministers didn't like them, perhaps a public competition could be held to find fresh designs. Weighing up the pros and cons, Treasury officials agreed that an open competition would make the public feel that they had the opportunity to contribute their ideas. It would also

Secret preparations 31

Opposite far left: Plaster model for a 1/2p featuring the Welsh Dragon by Christopher Ironside, 1963–6.

Opposite right: Plaster model for a 5p featuring the three crowns of the Order of Bath by Christopher Ironside, 1963–6.

Left: Plaster model for a 20p featuring the Royal Coat of Arms by Christopher Ironside, 1963–6.

enable designers who had felt left out to have their chance, in a more democratic manner than if the Mint simply invited selected artists to contribute, as it had sometimes done in the past. On the other hand, in a specialist field such as coin design, experience showed that most entries from the public were unviable. Moreover, the time required to run the competition could put the whole timetable at risk. Taking these factors into consideration, a compromise was reached: there would be an open competition run in parallel with a competition for selected invited artists, with the extremely tight deadline of 1 January 1967 for all entries. Artists who had contributed to the team projects were not invited to submit fresh designs, but their original ideas were automatically forwarded for reconsideration. Shortlisting would take place in the second week of January 1967 and judging in the third week. The RMAC was permitted to choose the winner, although Callaghan steered the decision by expressing a preference for designs featuring the Prince of Wales feathers, a Parliamentary design, Britannia and the Coat of Arms.

With the decision made, Jack James had the unenviable task of breaking the news to Ironside. According to Jean, having invited him to his office, James thrust an enormous gin and tonic in his hands with the words: 'Drink that. Callaghan is about to announce in the House of Commons that Britain will be going decimal but he insists there must be an open competition for the designs. Everyone who wants to must have a chance to enter. So, you haven't won after all.'[4]

The competition

Announced via press release in November 1966, the decimal design competition was open to all UK citizens and those of Commonwealth countries. By the closing date submissions from eighty-three entrants totalling almost 900 drawings had been received, although few were from overseas.

The submissions, which were displayed anonymously, were sorted by the judging committee into three groups: those by artists specially invited (sixteen in total), new designs by other artists who showed some skill in drawing and, in the third pile, designs by artists more crudely drawn. Submissions by artists known to the Mint included Humphrey Paget (1893–1974), whose portrait of George VI had previously featured on the UK coinage. His design for a 20p coin features the façade of Buckingham Palace. Paul Vincze (1907–94), an experienced sculptor and medallist who had designed numerous coins for Commonwealth countries, produced a series of striking images to represent modern Britain including Jodrell Bank observatory, a shirtless miner blasting a coal face, and the fast breeder reactor sphere at Dounreay power station. Jack James was perhaps thinking of Vincze's designs when he later remarked that 'those which are up to the minute now may soon

Left: A design by Paul Vincze for the decimal coinage featuring the fast breeder reactor sphere at Dounreay power station.

be outmoded, and they will not do'. Many more submissions feature traditional symbols such as shields, the lion passant (walking), coats of arms, as well as flora and fauna.

Leafing through these designs, the difference in quality between submissions by established artists and members of the public becomes apparent. Ignoring the competition's golden rule that 'less is more', one entrant, a Miss A.I.D. Dennis from Tunbridge Wells, could be commended if only for managing to squeeze a daffodil, leek, shamrock, thistle, rose, the denomination *and* a portrait of the Queen all on one side of her sketch for the 10p piece. Another entrant from New Zealand produced an imaginative landscape featuring St Paul's Cathedral and the recently completed BT Tower but noted that he wasn't sure what the latter landmark looked like. The result wouldn't look out of place in science fiction. One of the youngest entrants, a D Edwards, aged twelve, submitted a design for the 10p with remarkable prescience, as the Prince of Wales feathers is more or less drawn as it would eventually appear on the decimal 2p coin. Of course, non-established artists stood little chance against experienced designers, especially since all entrants were expected to be capable of turning their drawings into plaster models. The submissions nevertheless served a useful function in giving the public a voice. They remain interesting for the way they conservatively explore concepts of sovereignty and nationhood during what was supposed to be the swinging sixties.

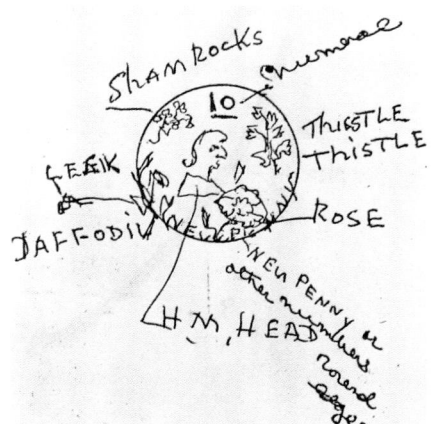

Left: Design for a coin by Miss A.I.D. Dennis.

34 Making Change

After a few days' despair, Ironside resolved that he must enter the open competition with an improved set of designs, so he went back to the drawing board. Apart from two days a week teaching he worked all day, every day, according to Jean, 'producing endless versions of lions, Britannias, dragons, coats of arms, St Georges and roses'. Three sets of designs emerged: Royal, Regional and Popular. The first two sets

Above and opposite: Ironside's entries (Sets 1–4) for the design competition, 1966.

feature exclusively heraldic imagery. The third set mixes heraldry and popular symbols such as the ship, representing Britain as an island. On impulse Ironside added a fourth 'Avant-Garde' set. Here a set of scales on the 1p symbolises equal rights, opportunities and obligations while a gyroscope on the 2p represents stability.

Left: Ironside's sketch for the ½p featuring the badge of Henry VII, a Portcullis, associated with Parliament, 1966.

Writing from Buckingham Palace on 23 January 1967, the Duke of Edinburgh informed Callaghan that a decision had been made. He had, he said, told the Advisory Committee that not all the coins had to be designed by the same person, but it had become apparent during the judging process that it was indeed possible to achieve a complete set of designs by one man: Christopher Ironside. 'In the course of discussion it turned out that the "Prince of Wales feathers" [favoured by the Committee] was designed by Ironside and he had also done a design incorporating the "Portcullis" which is the badge associated with Westminster and used by Members of Parliament.' His letter concludes, in typical bluntness, with a withering putdown of the coinage of other European countries:

> I took the opportunity of looking at the coins currently in use in Europe and I can assure you that we could not possibly do as badly as that.

Once more, Ironside's designs had stood up to scrutiny. Jean Ironside remembers sitting in the car outside a house party sometime in January 1967 when they heard that he had won. However, the wording of the communication was dispiritingly non-committal: 'your designs have been chosen for development', Ironside was told, an indication perhaps that the Mint was wary of falsely raising his hopes for a second time. In fact, he would have to wait until February 1968 for public confirmation that he was designer of the coin's reverses and was at one point advised that 'nothing is certain until the coins are finished and have received Royal Assent.'

The next phase in the development of the decimal reverses lasted through to the summer of 1967. Ironside worked with the RMAC over the development and modification of the new designs, sometimes by incremental changes, in order to satisfy the many varied views of the committee members. This was a stressful time in which Ironside admitted he'd had to set his own views, and ego as an artist, to one side and do his utmost to make the designs acceptable.

Above: This set of drawings from early 1967 shows the designs close to being finalised (apart from the 50p). Following feedback from the RMAC the chains on the portcullis on the 1p were straightened, the lion's tail on the 10p was thickened at the base and a crown was added to the thistle on the 5p.

Gradually, the designs began to fall into place – the crest of England on the 10p, badge of Scotland on the 5p and badge of the Prince of Wales on the 2p. The badge of Henry VII – the portcullis motif associated with Parliament – was originally intended for the ½p. However, since the ½p was likely to be later withdrawn owing to its decreasing purchase value, its design was considered the least important of the set. The decision was therefore taken to transfer the badge onto the 1p coin while a royal crown, a more dispensable design, was introduced on the ½p. The Mint was later alerted to a minor error in the badge of Henry VII, specifically the crown above the Portcullis where the cross pattée and not the fleur-de-lys should come by the arches. The same error had been made on the sixteenth century gates of Westminster chapel, which is possibly where Ironside saw and copied the design. Nobody else had seemed to notice, and so the Mint remained quiet.

Most controversial, perhaps, was the decision to drop Britannia, currently on the pre-decimal penny, from the new designs. Once again it had proven the hardest to get right. Jack James said that he regretted the omission of Britannia from the coinage but that, in a reference to the competition's brief requiring large numerals on the coins, 'apart

Above left: Ironside preferred to work on his plasters in reverse although even he, an experienced sculptor, sometimes made mistakes. On this model for the 1p he has cut the top of the numeral the wrong way around.

Above right: Plaster model for the 2p featuring the Prince of Wales feathers by Christopher Ironside, 1966–8.

from anything else the lady does not sit well over a large numeral. She would be very uncomfortable'. The chancellor provisionally accepted the new designs in September 1967 and the Palace approved them shortly before they were announced to the public on 15 February 1968, exactly three years prior to D-Day. The 5p and 10p coins went into circulation from April and were interchangeable with the 1*s.* and 2*s.* coins.

The 1966 government White Paper had rejected the Halsbury recommendation to introduce a 20p coin but paved the way for the introduction of a 50p coin. Its equivalent in the old system was the popular 10*s.* note. Introduced as a Treasury note in 1914, inflation had reduced its purchasing power in the subsequent decades, leading to a rise in the note's circulation. This in turn caused it to wear out more quickly, accounting for 20 per cent of all production by the Bank of England, but merely 4 per cent of the total value of the notes in circulation. Against these rising costs the Bank urged the government to replace the note with a coin, and the government consented. The £1, £5 and £10 notes would remain unchanged. About 200 million 10*s.* notes were in circulation, and the Mint aimed to produce 120 million 50p coins in time for the date of issue, October 1969. Given the potential controversy of replacing a note for a coin the government was keen that the transition should be as short as possible. But what should the 50p coin look like?

The White Paper recommended retaining the weight to value ratio of the coinage, meaning that the coins became heavier as they increased in value. This didn't necessarily present a problem except that the government had also determined that, to aid the transition, the 5p and 10p coins should be the exact same size and weight as their £.*s.d.* equivalent, the shilling and florin. This would have made the proposed 20p piece (later rejected) huge, and the 50p coin a pocket-splitting 55 grams (the issued coin weighed just 13½ grams). The government had already accepted one compromise proposed by the Halsbury Committee – a two-tiered system whereby the bronze coins corresponded to one weight system and the cupronickel coins to another. Now it must accept another – the introduction of a 50p piece, with a weight unrelated to either the bronze or cupronickel decimal coins. The White Paper sought to address this by announcing that a 50p piece should be significantly different in appearance from the other coins, 'elegantly designed' and 'popular as well as economically sound'. A different colour might help to distinguish it, but brass was the only real alternative and was, at the time, considered an unacceptably cheap alloy for such a high value coin (ironically, it would be later used as the principal alloy for the £1 coin, providing its distinctive golden hue). The only realistic option left was to make it in cupronickel. Given that its colour wouldn't distinguish it from the other decimal coins, the Mint looked at what else it could do to make the coin distinctive, and decided to experiment with its shape.

In early 1967 the Mint and DCB considered various suggestions, raising once again earlier proposals to create dish-shaped coins. A number of trial pieces were made in cupronickel and nickel, bearing Machin's portrait of the Queen and various reverses drawn from the pre-decimal coinage, but the coins were deemed too similar to the 10p piece and the differences in shape were insufficient to make it stand out. Abandoning the Halsbury recommendation that all the coins should be circular, the Mint decided to pursue the idea of a multi-sided coin. Odd-shaped coins had been produced before, notably in the 1930s with the introduction of the threepenny bit, although it had been a difficult coin to produce and Jack James admitted he was glad to see the back of it. Cash handling industries were initially consulted for their views on either a square, ten or twelve-sided coin, but the replies were unenthusiastic. Vending machine companies argued forcefully against such shapes as, in systems which operated by having the coins roll along a slot, this would inevitably lead to blockages.

Above: Bank of England 10s. note, 1963–66. The average lifespan of the note by the mid-1960s was just four or five months.

One technical advisor to the Board proposed an alternative – a shape of constant diameter but not a circle, in which each side had a slight curve to it. Such shapes had been used in rotary engines. The idea was passed to the Accessories Design Office at Bristol Siddeley, an aeronautical design company, which modified established formulas for the curvature of the lines until they came up with one that would work on any shape with odd sides of three or more. They recommended a seven-sided piece (technically speaking an equilateral-curve heptagon) making it not too irregular but not with too many sides that would make it resemble a circle. The new shape was passed through Perspex slots to demonstrate how it could roll down slopes, around corners and into a narrow slot.

Market research was carried out using square, seven, ten and twelve-sided prototypes. 200 housewives were approached and asked to investigate which of the four shapes could be most easily distinguished from the new decimal coins, both visually and by touch. The ten-sided piece performed the best, but the seven-sided piece came a close second. Tests with the cash handling industries found firmly in favour of the seven-sided shape. The square piece performed consistently the worst in all tests and was henceforth abandoned. Left with a choice, the Board weighted their decision in favour of the machine handling industries and concluded that the coin should be seven-sided.

> *It is difficult to get emotional over a piece of cupro-nickel whose shape is officially described as an equilateral curve heptagon.*
>
> **Patrick O'Leary, *The Times*, July 1969.**

With the shape all-but confirmed, Ironside commenced work on the reverse design. He produced a new drawing, favoured by the chancellor, that featured the Royal Coat of Arms. This design was developed beyond the summer of 1967. But then, in February 1968, came the public announcement of the new coins, minus the 50p (still in development) which elicited a public outcry over the omission of Britannia and lack of representation for Northern Ireland – 'Decimals displace Britannia', ran the headline in *The Times*. Ironside was asked to address these concerns by working up more ideas for the 50p.

Five alternatives followed – three were variations on the Royal Coat of Arms. One depicted Britannia and another was a floral design incorporating a shamrock, a nod to Northern Ireland that was quickly discarded as unsuitable.[5] For Britannia, Ironside revived a drawing from the second competition. As with all his Britannia designs, its development was fraught. On multiple occasions Ironside had Jean pose in various positions holding a ruler to recreate Britannia's trident. She also remembers an occasion when the RMAC asked Ironside to make Britannia lean back a fraction more, lifting the trident forward to prevent it from touching the lettering: 'impossible', she says, 'steam came out of Christopher's ears. Hours later, when I brought in the regulation mug of tea, the floor was covered with Britannias. "I've done it! Look at this", he cried. "Not exactly what they wanted but they will never know!" And they never did.'

The first coat of arms design was recognised as being the artistically better option, but the Mint recognised that Britannia would keep critics and the public happy. Tooling was worked up for both versions, providing the coat of arms version as an alternative should the latter be rejected at the last minute, or if technical issues coupled to the use of the relief on the new shape rendered it unfeasible. Trial strikes of the coins had not allayed Jack James' fears that the design would be unviable, particularly with regard to the life expectancy of the dies used to strike the coins. In search of a solution the Mint approached a French firm, Le Medailler, which was able to make the tooling in alloy instead of carbon steel, resulting in more durable dies.

Above: Copper halfpenny of Charles II, 1672. Britannia had been a regular feature on the coinage since the seventeenth century.

At the time it was introduced the 50p was the highest value coin to circulate since before the Second World War, and there were concerns about possible counterfeiting. To combat this, blanks were produced in metals of different weights and distributed to vending machine companies to help them to develop mechanisms to detect incorrectly weighted versions. The coin was produced to a very tight weight tolerance, tighter even than the other decimal coins. This came at a cost – the Mint had to ask permission from the Treasury to spend an additional £20,000 buying in cupronickel sheet at the required specification. Prior to its launch the coin was extensively marketed and the DCB arranged for the delivery of a sample to be used in the coin toss at the FA Cup Final held at Wembley on 26 April 1969. The toss

Above: Plaster model for the 50p by Christopher Ironside, 1967–8.

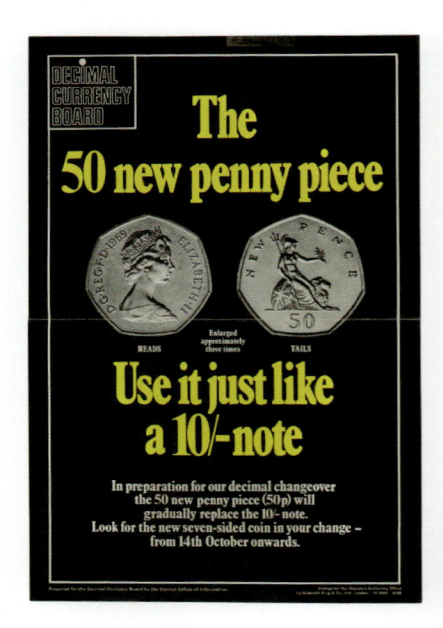

Left: 'The 50 new penny piece', DCB information poster, September 1969.

was won by Manchester City skipper Tony Book, whose team went on to beat Leicester City 1–0.

> *What I remember very clearly is an overwhelming sense of anti-climax as I gave my mum a 10s. note from my savings for her to change into the shiny new coins from the shop till. The 50p coin she gave me in return was, of course, completely accurate but rather prosaically singular for an excited nine-year old expecting an avalanche of silver. Perhaps that was the point of the public information campaign, after all. Not such a big deal.*
>
> **Kevin Ball, nine in 1971, living in Exeter.**

The coin went into circulation on 14 October 1969. Although initially positive, press coverage turned increasingly hostile in the ensuing weeks with *The Times* referring to the coin as a 'monstrosity' owing to its unusual shape, as well as concerns that it might be confused with the similarly sized 10p piece. The Mint received almost 600 letters of complaint, although only twenty-eight claimed to have lost money as a result of the confusion. Workers at a radio factory in Glamorgan refused to have their wages paid in the new coins, and in November it became the subject of a heated debate in the House of Commons. Despite this rocky start acceptance of the coin gradually grew, from a mere 28 per cent approval rating in November 1969 to 56 per cent by March 1970. In November of that year, the 10s. note was recalled.

The decimal reverses had the most protracted development of any coin series ever undertaken by the Mint and yet, despite many difficulties, Ironside had persisted with it from beginning to end. He would later describe the process as being like a jigsaw, with thousands of solutions. His achievement is all the more impressive considering that in the same period he designed the decimals for Tanzania (1966), Brunei (1967), Rwanda (1969), Jamaica (1969), Isle of Man (1970), Gibraltar (1971), Mauritius (1971) and Malta (1972). Ironside's UK decimals combined tradition and innovation, and Jack James declared himself to be highly satisfied with the outcome: 'we have concentrated on a simplicity of design – space and ease of reading. I personally think that as a result the series we have got would survive most comparisons.'

Left: Jack James (left) and Christopher Ironside examine a coin in a publicity photo. The two became close and in 1968 Ironside asked his friend 'Jolly Jack' to be godfather to his son Christian, who was christened with the middle name Decimus.

Left (top): UK ½ new penny coin reverse, 1971, featuring the royal crown.

Left (middle): UK 1 new penny coin reverse, 1971, showing a portcullis with chains royally crowned, being a badge of Henry VII and latterly associated with the Palace of Westminster, being used extensively as a badge of Parliament.

Left (bottom): UK 2 new pence coin reverse, 1971, featuring the badge of the Prince of Wales consisting of three ostrich feathers passed through a coronet with the motto *ICH DIEN* ('I serve').

The competition **47**

Left (top): UK 5 new pence coin reverse, 1968, featuring the badge of Scotland: a thistle royally crowned.

Left (middle): UK 10 new pence coin reverse, 1968, featuring the crest of England: a lion passant guardant (walking left, head facing the viewer), royally crowned.

Left (bottom): UK 50 new pence coin reverse, 1969, featuring a figure of Britannia, seated beside a lion, with a shield resting against her right side, holding a trident in her right hand and an olive branch in her left hand.

Exile from Tower Hill

The 1950s and 1960s were a boom time for the Mint as it won several large contracts to supply former British colonies with their post-independence currencies. These contracts, coupled with the anticipation of a large order for the UK decimal coinage, led senior Mint officials to consider how it could expand its operations to cope. The existing facility at Tower Hill, home to the Mint since 1810, was a building designed by James Johnson with neoclassical renovations by Sir Robert Smirke (1780–1867). It must have been abundantly clear to anyone who visited that this cramped site with its antiquated machinery would struggle to produce the estimated four billion new coins required for the UK to decimalise.

A solution of sorts presented itself through a 1963 report that recommended removing government activity from London to deprived areas of the UK suffering high levels of unemployment. Adoption of these recommendations, as well as a pressing need to modernise the Royal Mint, led to the decision in 1967 to construct a brand new facility beyond the capital. But where to build it? Anxious to appease

Above: The Tower Hill Mint as it appeared in the early 20th Century.

voters, MPs from all corners of the UK lobbied for the new facility to be built in their constituencies.

By March 1967, the list of possible sites had been narrowed to Llantrisant in South Wales, Cumbernauld in Scotland and Washington in North East England, all of which satisfied the government's dispersal criteria. Llantrisant emerged as the favourite, near to James Callaghan's Cardiff South East constituency and in an area where high unemployment was soon to be exacerbated by impending pit closures in the nearby Rhondda Valley. Mint management preferred Llantrisant because it was closest of the three sites to London, thus minimising the disruption to employees who chose to relocate and remaining accessible to overseas customers who, declared Jack James, 'could seldom be enticed up to Durham'. In April 1967 the Ministerial Committee on Environmental Planning formally approved the building of the new facility in Llantrisant and, in August, James arrived from London to commence the earthworks: 'I had the daunting pleasure', he said, 'of turning the first sod, in a monster weighing 27 tons'. With three years to go until D-Day, the foundation stone was laid at the Llantrisant site in February 1968. Behind it, in accordance with tradition, were placed two new decimal 2p coins. In the meantime, a temporary factory had opened

Above: This Associated Press photograph from February 1969 shows the new Llantrisant Mint 'from a safe distance, as security regulations require'.

at Bridgend, to which a small number of experienced staff transferred from Tower Hill to train the Welsh workforce. The Bridgend plant produced 250 million decimal ½p, 1p and 2p coins, while production of the 5p and 10p pieces remained at Tower Hill. Llantrisant was officially opened by the Queen in December 1968, and 1.4 billion coins were struck in its first year of operation. The decimal coins were struck a year ahead to allow the Mint to commence production of overseas coins.

Most Mint employees had previously been drawn from the London boroughs, many of whom had worked at the Tower Hill site for decades and in successive generations. Keen to retain experienced staff where possible, the Mint organised leisure trips to the new site in a bid to tempt experienced employees to relocate to this relatively unknown village ten miles outside Cardiff ('The Hole with the Mint', as it became disparagingly known). Albert Legrand, chairman of the Tower Hill union, was one of those who went on a tour: 'we got out of the coach at one place, and my wife said, "when's the next train back to London? I've left pit heaps once, and I'm not moving back to them."' Others were more open-minded. Muriel Cowley, who made the move with her husband, a chargehand electrician, had no regrets:

> Oh no, it's lovely here. We lived in a council flat in Sanderstead before we came to Bridgend and I don't think there's much in it as far as rent goes. We were paying £5 there five years ago, now we're paying £7. We had our pick of the council houses here and, in fact, we were taken around the one we had when we were on the tour they gave us from the Mint. We get out a lot more since we've been here, because it used to be so expensive in London, you can get through a week's wages in an evening up the West End.

About 400 employees remained at the Tower Mint as its activities were gradually wound down, about half of whom were made redundant when the site closed for good, in 1975. The old Mint was converted for office use and then sold to a developer with plans to turn it into a publicly accessible, car-free workspace with shops and cafes. However, in 2018 the site was reportedly sold to the People's Republic of China which announced it was turning the site into its new UK embassy, pending planning permission.

The Decimal Currency Board

Announcing decimalisation to Parliament on 1 March 1966, Callaghan stated that a Decimal Currency Board would be appointed to oversee the change, at first acting as an advisory body and then gaining full statutory function from July 1967. The DCB's remit was to facilitate transition to the new currency, deal with problems, promote arrangements to adapt machinery and equipment to handle the new currency, and to receive and consider requests for compensation in consequence of the changes.[6] Lord William 'Bill' Fiske (1905–75) was appointed its chair. Born in 1905 and educated at Berkhamsted Collegiate School, Bill Fiske had worked at the Bank of England and as a civil servant before his election as a Labour member of London County Council in 1946. He became first leader of the reformed Greater London Council (GLC) in 1964.

Left: Bill Fiske, chair of the DCB.

With a staff of about fifty, the Board was in no way equipped to take on full responsibility for the transition and as such it acted more as a facilitator, giving advice, information and publicity. Its strategy fell into three phases, firstly to reach out to large organisations in 1968–9, then retailers in 1969–70 and finally the general public in 1970–1. As Noel Moore (1928–2008), secretary to the Board, pointed out: 'there seemed no point in stimulating interest in an event that lay three or more years in the future.'

The DCB planned its campaign carefully. Over three and a half years it spent £2 million of public money on advertising, of which almost 75 per cent was spent in the period from December 1970 to February 1971. The DCB determined that information should be released sequentially, to slowly build knowledge among the populace.

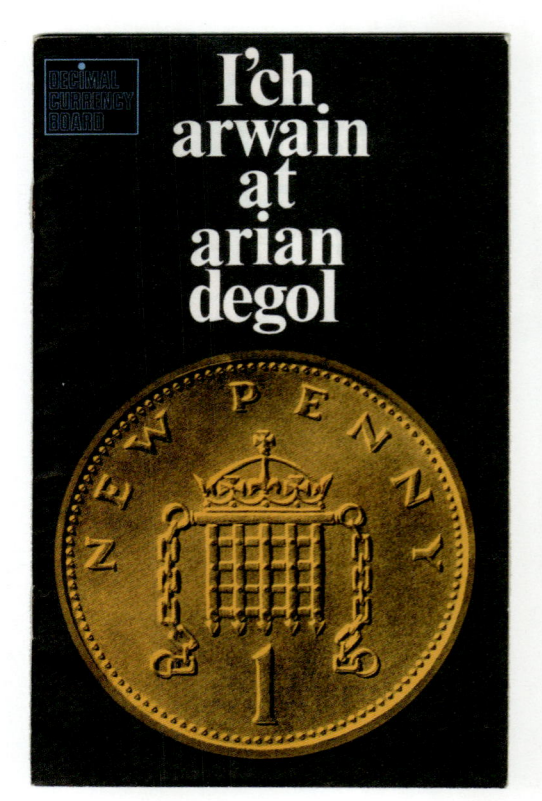

Left: The Welsh language edition of the DCB guide to decimal currency. This free twenty-one-page booklet was posted out to every household in Britain. An obvious disadvantage to this was that the DCB could not control who read it, or how many times.

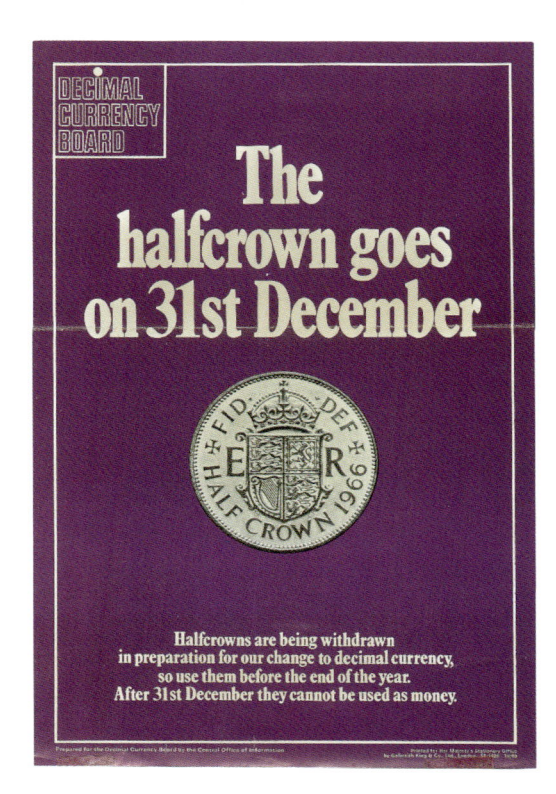

Left: 'The halfcrown goes on 31st December', DCB information poster, 1969. Besides promoting the new decimal coins the DCB alerted the public to the withdrawal of the old ones, arranging for 15 by 10 inch posters such as this to be displayed in all UK post offices.

In coordinating the public campaign it focused on three sequential elements, beginning with the effect of decimalisation on the coinage. Next would be its effect on shops and prices. The final part focused on the conversion between old and new money. These three points provided the structure of the final campaign.

To achieve market saturation, the DCB advertised in local and national newspapers, magazines, billboards and through TV advertising, hitting a peak between December 1970 and February 1971. Adopting a 'countdown' approach such as 'D-Day – seven weeks to go' down to 'Today is D-Day', a series of nine advertisements appeared across the UK newspapers, while magazine advertisements gave advice on shopping and cash handling. Six 30-second TV commercials accustomed the ear to the language of decimal pricing and to demonstrate shopping scenarios.

Altogether these commercials occupied 1,444 spots, one of the most concentrated campaigns ever to appear on independent television.

Elderly audiences, who had been identified as being least likely to adapt to the new currency, were targeted through advertisements in social welfare and religious publications. Fiske also recorded a three-minute message to be broadcast through the Post Office's popular Dial-a-Disc telephone information service, used by an estimated 150–200,000 people. Regular surveys of the public campaign were conducted, and the results fed back in so that the messaging could be modified on a weekly basis to address problem areas.

On TV and radio there were topical mentions in programmes such as *Coronation Street* and *The Archers*, while *Steptoe & Son*'s Wilfred Brambell and the comedian Max Bygraves both released songs to mark the occasion. Neither sold well. The DCB could not control the production of this content, per se, but it offered fact-checking and advice about how to present information. From early 1971 TV and radio networks began to broadcast decimal-themed programmes. BBC Radio Four devoted a half-hour episode of its popular *Study on Four* programme to decimalisation, and a series of shorts, *Decimal Five*, appeared on BBC TV featuring music by The Scaffold. On ITV there were repeated broadcasts of a half-hour drama, *Granny Gets the Point* starring Doris Hare, who was then appearing in the popular sitcom *On the Buses*. Granny Collins is an elderly curmudgeon living in a multi-generational household. Her initial response to decimalisation is anger, and she vows to give her decimalised pension money 'back to them, where it hurts!' Anger subsides into fear as she retreats to her bedroom in tears, where she has a surreal dream involving the milkman and decimal bullets firing from all sides. Suffice to say, Granny does eventually get the point. Having had the men of the house patiently explain it to her (challenging gender stereotypes wasn't within the scriptwriter's remit), she proudly shows off her knowledge to a startled group of younger shoppers when she next visits her granddaughter's boutique.

Needing little encouragement from the DCB, many manufacturers cashed in on decimalisation by producing a range of merchandise, memorabilia and practical items, some of which was useful, much of which was not. A range of decimal converters was made and sold. These usually consisted of a rotating disc displaying pre-decimal values on one ring, and on the other the price in decimal money. These were

The Decimal Currency Board 55

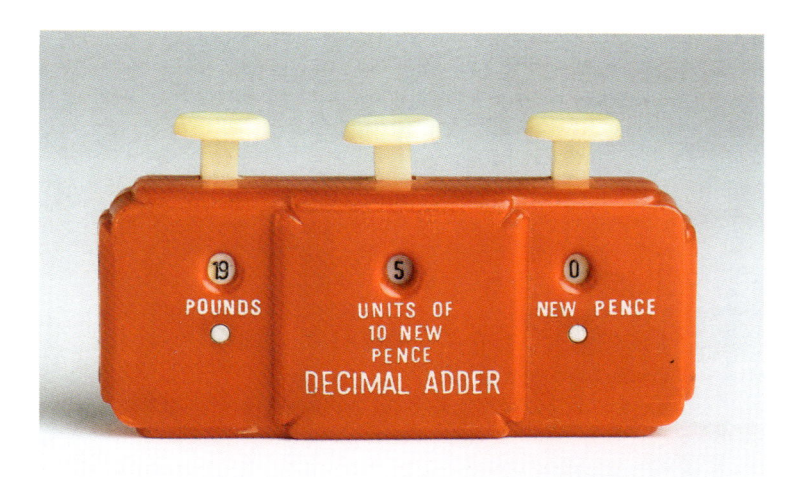

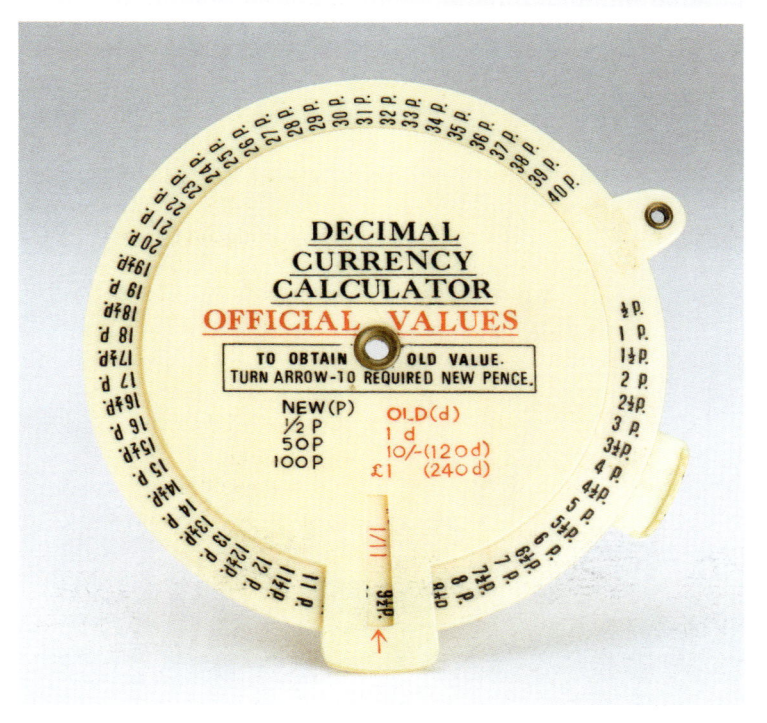

Above: Examples of the available decimal converters. Some worked better than others.

made in two different sizes – one for retailers to hang by a length of string at the shop counter, and smaller versions for customers' pockets. Some were counters in the form of little plastic boxes with clickers on the outside and internal cylinders that spun when clicked, which served little purpose except to demonstrate to users how to count in multiples of ten. Meanwhile, games manufacturers modified existing product lines such as dominoes or card games to feature a decimal theme. Waddingtons re-released an old title, *Sum-It*, updated as a decimal coin edition, while the reflex-based card game *Snip-Snap* (or, simply, 'Snap') was adapted to depict old and new money. The game was popular among teachers who used it as a fun way to educate school children about decimalisation.

The 'Shoppers' Table', the official conversion rate, featured on almost every conceivable item. Pottery manufacturers produced a range of rather dull-looking mugs with the table printed around the outside; Parker produced a pen with a decimal converter in the barrel, while tea towels were printed with images redolent of Britishness – the Routemaster bus and cups of tea, alongside images of grocery items and their decimal price, with the Shoppers' Table across the middle.

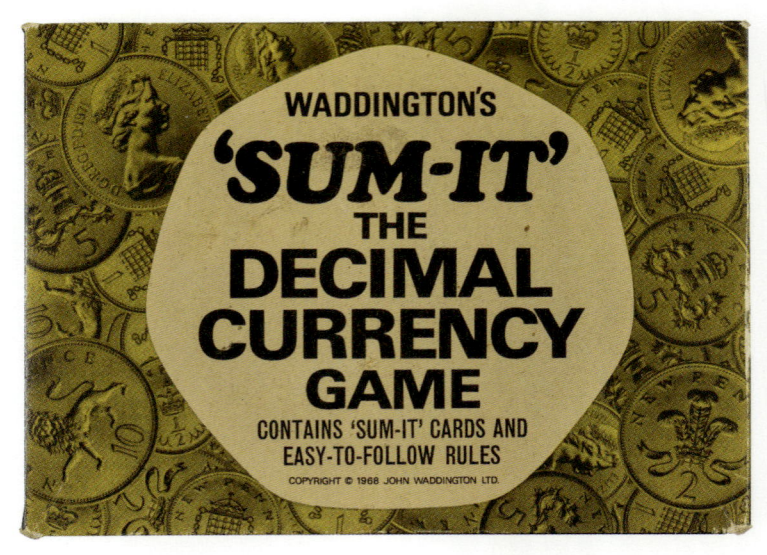

Above and opposite: 'Sum-it' The Decimal Currency Game, New Money Dominoes and *Snip-Snap,* about 1971.

The Decimal Currency Board 57

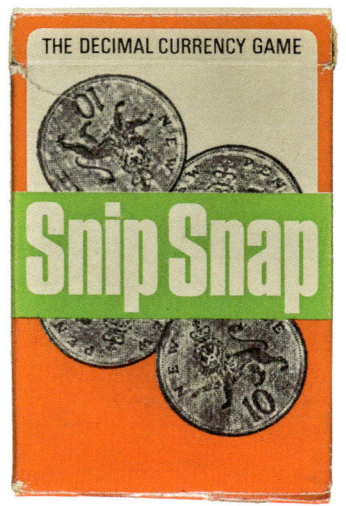

Above: Mug with the decimal conversion table printed around the outside, 1971.

58 Making Change

What made these products less useful was that the conversion table was merely a guide; retailers were encouraged, but not obliged to follow the exchange rate set by the DCB. Inevitably, soon after D-Day most of this bric-a-brac became redundant, pushed to the backs of drawers.

Above: A decimal tea towel, about 1968.

Right: Wooden money box with pictures of the new coins, 1968. Note that the design of the new seven-sided 50p had yet to be announced.

S.O.S.

There were several controversies surrounding decimalisation, from the selection of the pound as the main unit (in preference to the 10*s*.), to the initially furious public response to the 50p piece. Yet neither of these managed to galvanise public opinion as much as the decision to abolish the sixpence, as announced through the 1969 Decimal Currency Act. Under a 10-shilling system the sixpence's place as a 5-cent coin would have been taken for granted, but under a pound system it was worth 2½p, which was decidedly unconventional. The sixpence, or 'tanner' was, nevertheless, a very popular unit because it was used in many coin-operated machines such as parking meters, vending machines, in public telephones and on buses. Even the government had been split on the matter: the bill that went to the Lords abolished the coin, but a Lords amendment put it back in, only for the Commons to duly amend it again when it came back. This was the bill as it stood when it received Royal Assent on 16 May 1969. Given that the Act also removed the provision for compensation to businesses for the changeover, the abolition of the sixpence therefore increased the financial burden on companies for the cost of converting machines, and heightened the controversy surrounding its withdrawal.

Above: UK sixpence, 1967.

The primary concern to the public was inflation. Interviewees for a 1970 BBC news broadcast on the future of the coin, mostly comprising pensioners, complained that they would hate to see it dropped. One interviewee argued, not altogether convincingly, for retaining the sixpence 'for the simple reason is you come from Hammersmith to Goldhawk Road, for which you'll [now] have to pay a shilling. They're not so quick in putting your wages up, but all the prices and everything are going up and up and up!' Amid the outcry a 'Save Our Sixpence' campaign, or S.O.S. for short, was launched by the press.

> *Don't abolish it, please!*
> *I'd be most grateful!*
>
> **Interviewed by the BBC, a pensioner reacts to news that the tanner is to be abolished.**

Far from being concerned, however, Harold Wilson sensed an opportunity – a small sacrifice for a big win. If it gave ground on the sixpence, he reasoned, this would demonstrate the government's commitment to reducing inflation. In February 1970, less than twelve months prior to D-Day, the government announced that it was willing to reconsider its fate, opening the door for a Parliamentary debate. Jumping the gun by some margin, the *Daily Mail* declared the coin to have been saved. Finally, in April 1970 the chancellor, Roy Jenkins (1923–2003), announced a reprieve: the

Above: A 'Save Our Sixpence' campaign sticker.

Our Sixpence CAMPAIGN

sixpence would remain legal tender, valued at 2½p, for at least two years after D-Day.

The announcement was undoubtedly a sop to critics of decimalisation, but it had worked. It came at no cost to the government, which could simply sit back, do nothing and wait for the public to judge whether they wished to keep using the coin. As things turned out, the sixpence quickly fell out of use. Production of new coins for circulation had been suspended after 1967 and by a couple of years after D-Day it accounted for only a tiny percentage of transactions. It remained current tender until 1980 when it was withdrawn, principally so that the government could reclaim the £3.5 million locked into its metal value. Making the decision, Margaret Thatcher (1925–2013) declared to her chancellor, Geoffrey Howe (1926–2015), that 'there will be headlines about the end of the tanner – but for £3.5 million it will be worth it'. In fact, this time the public were quite sanguine about its withdrawal, and the announcement generated a mere dozen letters of complaint.

A national effort

If proof were needed that decimalisation required a national mobilisation, then it lay with the thousands of companies and retailers who employed or redeployed staff to make their organisations decimal-ready. Some companies were just starting to move their files onto computers, which meant that all their accounting programs had to be updated to reckon in pounds and pence. Richard Fuller was lead programmer at Grindlays Bank in London. The bank, he recalls, had bought an English Electric KDF6 computer for £60,000, an exorbitant sum, back in 1964. His team was tasked with amending existing programs to cater for both £.s.d. and decimal amounts and, at conversion, to add a statement line showing the change on customer accounts. By September 1970 the conversion programs had been completed, tested and were ready to go. 'In almost forty years of working with IT systems', he says, 'this is the only project that was ever finished ahead of time and within budget.'

At Greater London Council, trainee systems analyst Rachel Terry was assigned to the new two-person decimalisation team in the

Above: A Lloyds Bank customer account statement, February 1971.

Treasurer's department. 'Each computer file', she says, 'of which there were about eighty at the time, had to have all sterling fields reformatted and recalculated before the updated program could be run.' She and a colleague used punched cards for the input in machine language, marking the slots on each card in soft dark pencil. The cards were then punched in a data preparation room.

Other organisations put their staff to work amending or converting physical records. Fresh out of school, Tony McMahon was living in Birmingham in 1970 where he was employed as a junior clerk by the Federated Employers Insurance Company. After a brief introduction to various staff members he was presented with several large ledgers which contained details of claims recorded with payment details in £.s.d., which all had to be converted to decimal currency. 'There was no calculator!' says Tony, but 'it was assumed that as I had just left school with an O level in Mathematics, I was ideally suited to this particular job. I'm not really sure how long it took me to complete this task, but I was probably still doing it on 15 February 1971!' John Miller, W.S., performed a similar task at a solicitor's in Edinburgh, where he was assigned the job of converting the transactions on the accounts of hundreds of trust or executory estates. 'I hated doing these accounts', he says, 'it was a tedious job at the best of times to track every transaction to the exact old penny, but decimalisation not only doubled the work (for obvious reasons) but also threw up discrepancies where old money would not convert exactly into new money. The resulting compromises, whilst of no real financial consequence, perhaps hastened the end of these kind of Accounts, and introduced the world of "near enough" – thank goodness!'

Accountants were particularly busy and all but the biggest firms still used physical ledgers. Reg Holmes was employed at a chartered accountancy firm in London where, in between meetings with clients, he had to update the balances so that they would be shown in new money. 'The net result', he says, 'was that by December 1970 we had done so many of these conversions we could do it in our head without thinking about it. We became very popular at home and in shops for weeks after 15 February. As others fumbled with their conversion charts we helped by telling them what the amount was in old and new money.'

The UK's estimated 610,000 cash registers all had to be made decimal-ready. The two main brands were Sweda, from Sweden and, with a marginally bigger market share, the National Cash Register company (NCR) based in Dayton, Ohio, USA. Planning had commenced years in advance, detailed inventories had been made of the number of each model in operation and parts had been stockpiled ready for the changeover. Newer part-electric models were simpler and could be adapted by replacing a few easily accessible components. Most machines made after 1960 were already decimal-ready, meaning that they could be converted at the flick of a switch. Older models were more complicated – some models, for example, dated back to the turn of the century. These mechanical models had to be taken to pieces to have their cylindrical mechanisms modified or replaced altogether.

The conversion of this equipment came at a cost which had to be borne by the retailer. Sainsbury's estimated the total cost of the

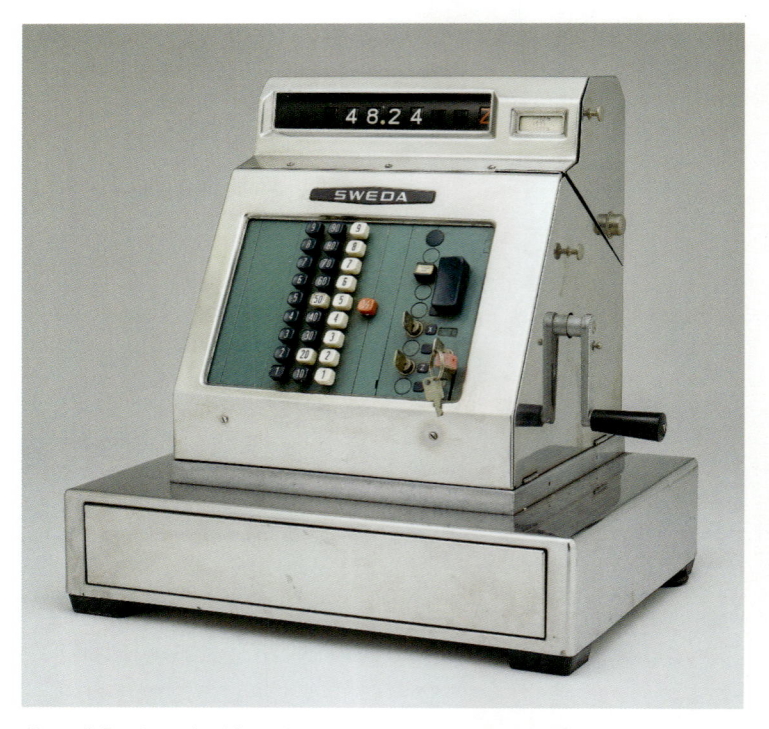

Above: A Sweda model 46 stainless steel cash register, about 1960, converted to decimal. For conversion to decimal this model required the replacement of part of its keyboard.

changeover, including the conversion of 3,000 cash registers, 1,500 sets of scales and all its accounting machinery, to be £325,000. Some retailers used decimalisation as an opportunity to scrap their older machines, replacing them with decimal-ready tills. Yet with new machines costing about £100, this was a costly option and most elected to have their existing machines converted, at a cost of £30 or £40 per machine. The task fell to teams of technicians employed by the big manufacturers who, because many retailers had left it to the last moment to book in their conversion, had to work around the clock from January to around October 1971, working fifty or even sixty-hour weeks. NCR alone employed 1,600 technicians to complete the job. In the meantime, smaller retailers improvised, many following DCB advice to use their tills as a cash only drawer until they could have them converted. Yasmin Ali remembers that her mother had an old Victorian cash register in their shop in Birmingham: 'I recall that she took to using mental arithmetic for all transactions, and opened the till using the key labelled either "No Sale" or "No Charge" – basically a key without a number in pounds, shillings or pence.'

In terms of preparedness few could match Sainsbury's, at the time Britain's largest grocer which, in February 1970, converted its Croydon store to serve as a decimal training shop. The opening was attended by Bill Fiske, Jennifer Jenkins (chair of the Consumers' Association and wife of Roy Jenkins, chancellor of the exchequer) and representatives of various women's organisations. The shop aimed to provide as realistic a shopping experience as possible in which to train 1,500 Sainsbury's employees (out of a total staff of 25,000). Its customers were groups from women's organisations who were asked to rate their experience. Upon arrival they were shown a short film, *Quick Change*, and then allowed to try shopping in the store, which stocked around 400 of Sainsbury's 3,000-strong product line. The consumer magazine *Which?* interviewed sixty-seven housewives who had just been through the store, and the results were encouraging: overall, sixty-two of the group rated the experience as at least 'fairly easy'.

Large stores and retail businesses carried out extensive employee training. Fred Tyler, Saturday boy at Tesco in Northampton, was tasked with training other till staff:

66 Making Change

Above: Sainsbury's decimal shop in Croydon, 1970.

> We had training sessions in the late afternoon when I got there from school in the two weeks running up to D-Day. We did not have the coins until the day, so we had to make do with cardboard money; it was just like playing at post offices and shops! The staff were very good and the process seemed almost a waste of time when it came to dealing with decimal currency.

Smaller chains and independent shops couldn't afford to hire extra staff, so their arrangements were more ad hoc. Myma Fahie ran the old family butchers with her husband in a small town on the Essex coast. Their biggest challenge, she says, 'was not being able to purchase fancy new scales, so we had to find a way of dealing with the change in money. This fell to me and I spent several days working out the prices shown on our old scales and covering each price with a small sticky label showing the equivalent in the decimal coinage. We never did get around to buying a new set of scales.'

In schools, decimalisation was made part of the curriculum. Penina Bowman was at primary school, as she remembers, 'we had cardboard coins to use in play transactions. I particularly remember we were taught to sing a song about it set to the tune of 'The 12 Days of Christmas.'' The run-up to D-Day made eight-year-old Yvonne Gallagher quite a star at her West London primary school – her dad was a pub manager with Watneys, and so she took one of the staff training kits to show her friends which had real specimen coins in it. Teaching decimalisation could be a tedious experience, as the curriculum largely required pupils to do calculations such as 'what would two pounds, three shillings and sixpence be in the new money?' This needlessly complicated the transaction – in time most people stopped doing the conversion altogether.

Opinion polls conducted between 1961 and 1971 had routinely put the public in favour of decimalisation, in principle if not in the detail. Leading up to D-Day the DCB's own surveys generally gave positive feedback about levels of public awareness, yet these contrasted sharply with press opinion pieces and commissioned investigations. A headline in *The Sun* at the beginning of February 1971 said that '4 in 10 people still don't get the point'. Published a week before D-Day, a *Guardian* investigation found that the information campaign had had limited effect on the public. Other scare stories emerged, such as people stockpiling food so that they wouldn't have to handle the new money, and criticism of the new ½p which, it was claimed, was so small that it would be easily lost. The press also gave extensive coverage to a peripheral organisation, the 'Anti-Decimal Group', which had been formed in 1969. Describing its crusade as like a resistance in an occupied country, it had corresponded with about 500 members of the public telling them to boycott the decimal currency. Against this onslaught, the DCB remarked to its dismay that the press was almost gleefully anticipating some sort of national meltdown on 15 February.

A more significant setback was a Post Office strike which resulted in the non-delivery of about five million (25 per cent) of the DCB booklets intended for UK households. This forced the DCB to spend an extra £78,000 on an emergency ad campaign, leading the *Daily Mail* to predict 'Trouble in store for D-Day'. Bill Fiske, however, remained unperturbed and confidently predicted that D-Day would be the non-event of 1971. By and large, he was right.

D-Day

Interviewer: No sentimental feelings about £.s.d.?
Interviewee: No, certainly not. I think if I had six fingers on each hand it might be a different story.

Associated Press interview with member of the public, 15 February 1971

To many UK households waking up on Monday 15 February 1971, it was a grey drizzly winter's day like any other: Edward Heath (1916–2005) was prime minister, the post office strike dragged on, and George Harrison's 'My Sweet Lord' was still number one in the charts. February had been chosen for the changeover because it was

Left: Front page of the *Daily Mirror*, 15 February 1971.

the least inconvenient time of the year – a quiet day for businesses and banks. Banks had, in fact, been closed since the end of Wednesday 10 February, giving them four days to prepare – an inconvenience for customers that was offset slightly by a recent innovation on the high street: the cashpoint. These had remained open over the weekend. Beyond taking delivery of the remaining decimal coins (the new ½p, 1p and 2p), a logistical challenge in itself, banks were required to clear all cheques in pre-decimal amounts, a procedure that was nicknamed 'Operation Checkpoint'. Describing it as 'the biggest single operation

Above top: London bus advertisement. London Underground and British Rail had gone decimal a day early, Sunday being quieter for travel than Monday.

Above: Bill Fiske, chair of the DCB, goes shopping, 15 February 1971.

ever undertaken in the history of British banking', the Royal Bank of Scotland's head office kept its staff canteen open twenty-four hours in the days leading up to D-Day, providing round-the-clock sustenance to its clearing department.

To the public, the most noticeable difference was on the UK's high streets – in shops, bars and restaurants. At the newsagents, a bag of Cadbury's chocolate buttons no longer cost sixpence, but 2½p. A pint of mild in the pub went from an average 2*s*. 11*d*. to 14½p, while two fish and chip dinners at a roadside Little Chef now cost 50p, from 10*s*. previously. Some retailers noted that they were slightly busier than usual for a Monday, attributing this to people wanting to try out the new currency. To curious shoppers the DCB offered two pieces of advice: if in doubt, pay more and receive more in change, and to pay in 6*d*. lots in old money. At 2½p, sixpence was the smallest amount that was easily convertible into decimal currency.

Department stores had extra staff working on the shop floor assisting customers with the changeover and being generally helpful. Harrods, for example, introduced 'Decimal Penny', which the company magazine described as 'a highly trained adviser available in most departments, to deal with all queries, difficulties or any out of the way problems which may arise.' Wearing sashes and straw hats to

Left: Sue Chotipong (née Smart) dressed as a 'Decimal Penny' at Harrods, February 1971.

increase their visibility, they were there to greet Bill Fiske during his brief stopover at the store on Valentine's Day.

Independent shops couldn't afford extra staff or specialist training, but they were equally important to ensure a smooth transition. In West Norwood, twenty-four-year-old TV cameraman David Beer spent D-Day in his dad's shoe repair shop, trying out his new sound recorder. In taped conversations between David's father, Jim, and his customers, he passes the time of day chatting about the changeover. 'It means I'll have to dig up the floorboards, get rid of all the old stuff!' jokes Jim, his voice punctuated by sounds of the cobbler's hammer. Listening to these recordings it becomes apparent that Jim's conversations are not simply transactional; he performs a pivotal role asking how his customers are 'bearing up' and dispensing informal advice. He is more knowledgeable about the coins and conversion rates than his customers, though he is careful not to lecture them. Although some are clearly confused by the new money, one or two of his male customers clearly enjoy showing off their mental arithmetic. Just as the bigger stores set up cash exchange counters, Jim's shop acts as an unofficial exchange, in which he puts through small purchases or sometimes none at all just so that an intrigued public can get their hands on the new coins. A schoolboy enters, half-heartedly enquiring the price of a

Above: Jim Beer at his shoe repair shop in West Norwood, late 1960s.

couple of items but clearly angling to just swap his old coins for new. 'How much do you want?' asks Jim. 'Erm, I got two bob on me now', replies the boy. Jim, pointing to some 2p coins, asks 'how many of these do you want for 2*s.*?' The schoolboy hesitates then answers slowly, unsure, '2*s.*? That's, erm…that's 10…pence?' '10 new pence,' says Jim affirmatively, and holding out a handful of 2p coins he asks, 'how many is that?' The boy hesitates again, 'Err…', and Jim mocks him, 'You're a schoolboy, you should know all this!' He proceeds to give him a short course in the decimal coinage. 'Now,' he says, giving the boy five 2p coins in exchange for his 2*s.*, 'how much is your bus fare?' One can imagine similar conversations up and down Britain's high streets as a nation of shopkeepers fulfilled a vital public function.

A survey commissioned by the DCB on the day found that 67 per cent of those interviewed found shopping easy, 25 per cent found it hard and 8 per cent had no feelings either way. Crucially, of those interviewed, 73 per cent said it would get easier over time. Newspapers were quick to declare that D-Day had been a success: 'You're getting the point', said London's *Evening Standard*. Notably, only two of the ten national newspapers led with a D-Day story. 'Lord Fiske was right', said *The Economist*, it was turning out to be a non-event.

The new system gradually bedded in. Robert Alfandary was Deputy Manager at the Sutton branch of Woolworths on D-Day and remembers how the store was just moving into electric tills:

> All goods were dual priced and there were two tills per counter, one in pounds, shillings, pence and the other decimal coinage. Depending on how payment was made it would be rung up in one till or the other. In week one customers could pay and receive change in either currency, and we in turn would use the applicable till. In week two, three and four the customer could pay either currency but would only receive change in decimal coins. From week five onwards, decimal was the only option, however, if for any reason the customer did not wish to exchange monies at the bank, we offered a service from the store office. Yes, there were the occasional moaners, but at the end of the day there was not a lot of choice.

At the Ely branch of Woolworth's, fourteen-year-old Pauline Tambling worked as a Saturday girl. There were two members of staff on every counter to explain to customers how the prices were set and to assure them that they were getting a fair conversion rate: 'there was plenty of time to talk to customers about the system and we were given guidance about what to say', she recalls.

> *My obsession was buying toy cars. Usually I got Matchbox ones, which were cheaper, but my dream was to buy the much bigger Dinky Toys, which cost 7s. and sixpence. I seemed to be perpetually saving up my pocket money to buy one of these and never quite having enough. In new money a Dinky Toy was 37.5p. Somehow that seemed a bit disappointingly small. 7s. and sixpence was a lot! That was the effect of decimalisation, that you would think 'that is not much' and then work it out in your head and think: 'Gosh, in old money that would have been EIGHT SHILLINGS' (or whatever).*

Peter Conway, nine in 1971, living in Winchester.

Above: A Dinky Triumph Spitfire toy car, 1971.

Old habits die hard and, as predicted, younger people who had spent fewer years living with £.s.d. adapted to the change the most easily. Decimalisation made life much easier for twelve-year-old Sharmann Quinn as well, who was working in McGuffins paper shop in Donaghadee, Northern Ireland, as she had only relatively recently moved from South Africa which had a decimalised rand: 'I found pounds, shillings and pence difficult and was glad to see the end of it', she says. Naturally, there were exceptions. Janet Taylor was ten on D-Day. She recalls being rather apprehensive, not being great at maths: 'I decided that as I knew the old sixpence was 2½ new pence, and that was the price of a little bag of Maltesers, then that's what I would buy at the corner shop because I was sure of the exchange!' Thirty-one-year-old John Prince had been in Hong Kong for three years serving in the RAF. As he recalls, he had not long become accustomed to the Hong Kong dollar:

> Getting back home it became mental torture because my mind just couldn't accept the new decimal coinage at face value. There followed about six months of converting decimal into the Hong Kong dollar and then to the good old reliable £.s.d. for every penny, whether old or new, I spent. Even my elderly grandparents were well ahead of me in coming to decimal terms!

There remained a delay with certain changeovers, particularly of slot machines. Andrew Pouteaux was an undergraduate in Coventry on D-Day. His clearest recollection is that notices were pinned to all the city centre public toilets which remained closed because the slot machines had yet to be converted.

Overall, D-Day had gone even more smoothly than expected. Its success enabled the changeover period to be significantly shortened, from eighteen months to just six. On 1 September 1971 the remaining pre-decimal coins were demonetised, and the UK currency was now fully decimal. The DCB's activities were quickly scaled back. By the Friday after D-Day many of its fifty-strong staff had already cleared their desks at the Board's offices on Northumberland Avenue. It was formally wound up in 1972.

Aftermath

I remember, when a pound was still a pound,
Twenty fags were one and threepence, 12 and a ½p
was half a crown,
Dolly Mixtures were our favourite little sweets,
I used to buy a bag for tuppence, and now they're 2p each.

The Barron Knights, 'Remember (Decimalisation)', 1978.

'Remember (Decimalisation)', the Barron Knights' tongue-in-cheek ode to pre-decimal Britain, was released seven years after D-Day, but much had changed. The 1950s and 1960s had seen the economy expand (albeit at a rate more sluggish than Britain's rivals), and unemployment rarely rose above 3 per cent. In the same period standards of living significantly improved, as more households became dual earners and a greater range of consumer goods became affordable. One in seven households had a television in 1951; by 1960 this was two-thirds. The 1970s, by contrast, witnessed an undeniable deterioration. Although it had already begun, Britain's decline as a manufacturing power became starkly apparent as the decade wore on. Successive governments had to contend with labour disputes, high inflation and rising unemployment. The 1973 Arab-Israeli War increased oil prices by 400 per cent, leading to shortages, a state of emergency and the three-day week.

On the one hand, decimalisation had undoubtedly gone smoothly, delivered on-time and within budget. However, and although it could scarcely be held accountable, the decimal currency became a conduit for criticism, a metaphor for the UK's loss of status. Indeed, as a perceived tipping point it was probably surpassed only by the unfavourable terms of Britain's entry to the European Economic Community (EEC) in 1973. Some commentators have even attempted to link the two events. Writing in the *Daily Mail* on the fortieth anniversary of D-Day in 2011, Dominic Sandbrook said that decimalisation had caused Britain to lose 'a little bit of our national soul'. D-Day, he explained, was a 'profoundly symbolic moment, marking the end of a proud history of defiant insularity and the beginning of the creeping Europeanisation of Britain's institutions.

Decimalisation was imposed from on high, the edict handed down by a political and intellectual elite indifferent to the romantic charms of history and tradition, but determined to turn Britain into a modern European state'.

The 'romantic charms' of the pre-decimal coinage may have inspired nostalgia, yet practical adherence to £.s.d. remained a minority hobby. The tiny pockets of resistance that remained were snuffed out as stubborn retailers found they were losing money. Other critics registered their contempt for the new coins by physically defacing them, such as by punching a cent symbol, '¢' to obliterate the 'p' for pence, or by stamping their pre-decimal value across the 5p and 10p coins. Britain's churches were unhappy with the 10p for a different reason – collection plates were now mostly filled with them rather than the old half-crown, which had been worth more.

The broader fear among members of the public had been that decimalisation would cause prices to go up. Some unscrupulous retailers may have taken the opportunity to round up prices (the DCB's 'Shoppers' Table' was only a guide, after all) but these were, by and large, isolated instances. Bill Fiske countered such claims by urging shoppers to boycott offending retailers but, stressed the DCB, 'the majority of shopkeepers are playing fair'. Indeed, the only major press article about prices going up in D-Day week involved pub

Left: Defaced 1973 10p coin, '2 SHILLING'.

jukeboxes, which strongly suggests a headline in search of a story. Sainsbury's, meanwhile, insisted that it had rounded down more than it had rounded up, so overall the customer was slightly better off. The evidence for wholesale inflation as a result of decimalisation is, at best, inconclusive: inflation remained steady at around 10 per cent throughout 1970–1, and only ramped up during the 1973–4 oil crisis. For comparison, during the Winter of Discontent, 1978–9, it peaked at 25 per cent.

Inflation did come to have an impact on the coinage, causing a year-on-year reduction in their purchasing power. A 20p coin was introduced in 1982 to alleviate pressure on the 5p and 10p coins, and the halfpenny, never a wildly popular coin in the first place owing to its small size, was withdrawn in 1984. A £1 coin was issued from 1983, replacing the £1 note, and a £2 coin from 1997. According to recent estimates the 1p has become the lowest value coin (in terms of purchasing power) in UK history, rendering its place in the currency more symbolic than practically useful.

> *In modern sculpture the contemporary idiom tends to be graphic rather than sculptural. I wanted to be traditional as far as possible. I was not designing for myself, but for everyone else. I feel fairly certain that in fifty years' time the coins will look very sixty-ish, but that cannot be helped.*
>
> **Christopher Ironside.**

Despite some comments at the time that the designs were old fashioned, Ironside's designs are now regarded as classic examples of good design: traditional and yet elegant, clear and uncluttered.[7] Apart from the removal of the 'New' in 'New Penny' and a later reduction in the size of the 5p, 10p and 50p the decimal reverses remained otherwise unchanged until 2008.[8] In that year an overhaul resulted in a series designed by Matthew Dent (b. 1981) showing different parts of the Royal Shield. Ironside's reverses continue to remain popular and are regularly revived on special edition coins. His unused design for the 50p featuring the Royal Coat of Arms was given a belated release in 2013 to commemorate the centenary of his birth, and Britannia reappeared on a 2019 50p celebrating fifty years since its first issue. It is fitting, therefore, that as decimalisation recedes in the public memory, the last word should go to Ironside. Reflecting on his achievement in 1969, he said this:

> The work of a great many artists who are geniuses is never recognised and probably eventually disappears. But if one is a coin designer, one's work lasts possibly long after death, everyone becomes familiar with it and it forms a small part of the history of the country for which it was designed, and one becomes famous. Not because one is a genius, or a saint or a monster, but simply because one is a coin designer.

Endnotes

1 With its currency pegged to sterling, the Republic of Ireland ultimately decided to follow the UK's lead.
2 Alec Douglas-Home, UK prime minister, to Reginald Maudling, chancellor of the exchequer, in 1963.
3 This according to John Rimington, assistant secretary to the Halsbury Committee.
4 Although, as noted above, it was the Duke of Edinburgh who suggested an open competition, albeit reluctantly. The conversation must have happened later than Jean remembers, perhaps in October 1966.
5 A specially designed 2p coin featuring the Red Hand of Ulster was considered for Northern Ireland, but the idea was later shelved.
6 The amended Decimal Currency Bill removed this latter requirement.
7 One critic sniped that they were more suited to 1902 than 1972.
8 Machin's portrait of the Queen was replaced in 1985.

Above: UK 50p coin, 2013, featuring a previously unused Ironside design, the Royal Coat of Arms.

Select Bibliography

The definitive account of decimalisation (although now regrettably hard to find in print copy) is the official Treasury history by Noel Moore, secretary to the Halsbury Committee and later the Decimal Currency Board. A thorough survey of the design of the coins and their critical reception is provided by Mark Stocker in his book *When Britain Went Decimal: The Coinage of 1971*, Spink Books, 2021. Recollections by Jean Ironside about Christopher Ironside and the design of the coins feature in the Royal Mint publication *Fleur de Coin Review*. Several academic studies and articles have explored aspects of decimalisation. Special mention goes to Andrew Cook's PhD thesis which provides a comprehensive analysis of the political developments that led to decimalisation, 1955–71. The author is further grateful to Chris Barker for sharing his unpublished history of the 50p coin, delivered as a lecture to the Royal Numismatic Society. The archives of the Royal Mint Museum in Llantrisant hold the submissions to the design competition, tooling for all the coins, minutes of RMAC meetings and other correspondence, duplicates of which are in the National Archives. Drawings and plaster models for the coins by Christopher Ironside are held in the British Museum, which also has an archive of personal reminiscences of D-Day compiled in 2020 following a call out in the *Financial Times*. Several of those respondents are quoted in this book.

Chris Barker, *London to Llantrisant: 50 Years of the Royal Mint in Wales* (Royal Mint, 2017).

Thomas V. Bonoma, 'Case 13. Program Management III: Decimalization of the Currency in Great Britain', in *Managing Marketing: Text, Cases, and Readings* (Collier MacMillan, 1984), pp.240–263.

Andrew Cook, *Britain's Other D-Day: the Politics of Decimalisation* (PhD thesis, University of Huddersfield, 2020).

Select Decimal Currency Board leaflets: 'Britain's New Coins'; 'Cash transactions during the changeover'; 'Conversion of accounting records'; 'Temporary adaptations of machines'; 'New money in your shop'; 'Your guide to decimal money' (all published by HMSO).

Catherine Eagleton, 'Christopher Ironside and the designs for the decimal coinage' in *Designing Change: the Art of Coin Design*, ed. Kevin Clancy (Royal Mint, 2008), pp.22–37.

Select Government papers: 'Report of the Committee of Inquiry on Decimal Currency - the Halsbury Report' (HMSO, 1963); 'Decimal Currency in the United Kingdom' (Government White Paper: Cmnd. 3164., 1966); 'The Decimal Currency Act 1967'; 'The Decimal Currency Board Currency Act 1969'.

Jean Ironside, 'Don't run up a flag', *Fleur de Coin Review*, 12 (February 1997), pp.7–9.

Arnold Machin, *Artist of an Icon: the Memoirs of Arnold Machin* (Frontier Publishing, 2002).

Noel Moore, *The Decimalisation of Britain's Currency* (HMSO, 1973).

Noel Moore, 'Decimal Coinage: a Mysteriously Inflammatory Subject', *Fleur de Coin Review*, 9 (January 1995), pp.4–6.

Mark Stocker, *When Britain Went Decimal: The Coinage of 1971* (Spink Books, 2021).

W.D & H.O Wills, *Decimal Currency for Retailers in Tobacco* (Premiums in Print, 1970).

Acknowledgements

With thanks to Chris Barker, Bobby Birchall, Claudia Bloch, Robert Bracey, Kevin Clancy, Andrew Cook, Lydia Cooper, Peter Dijkhuis, Michael Driver, Graham Dyer, Amanda Gregory, Bethany Holmes, Emma Howard, Maria Howell, Abigail Kenvyn, Olivia Marshall, Joe Richards, Mark Stocker, Sarah Tyley, Sebastian Wormell, and all the respondents to the British Museum's public request for decimalisation memories, advertised through the *Financial Times*, February 2020. Photography of British Museum objects has been provided by David Agar, Michael Rowe, Bradley Timms and John Williams.

Picture credits

All British Museum objects are © The Trustees of the British Museum, courtesy the Department of Photography and Imaging. Registration numbers and acquisition details of British Museum objects are included below. You can find out more about these objects and others in all areas of the British Museum's collection on the Museum's website at britishmuseum.org. The publisher would like to thank the copyright holders for granting permission to reproduce the images illustrated. Every attempt has been made to trace accurate ownership of copyrighted images in this book. Any errors or omissions will be corrected in subsequent editions provided notification is sent to the publishers.

Inside cover: Reproduced by permission of the Christopher Ironside OBE estate. 2006,0601.143; imprint page: Reproduced by permission of the Christopher Ironside OBE estate. 2006,0601.165; p. 10 1855,0321.14; p. 11 1994,0915.767; p. 12 Bequeathed by Thomas Bryan Clarke-Thornhill. 1935,0401.8576; p. 14 Bequeathed by Thomas Bryan Clarke-Thornhill. 1967,0104.14; p. 17 PA Images / Alamy Stock Photo. British Museum Coins & Medals Archive; p. 21 © Estate of the artist. 2019,4032.101, 2019,4032.114; p. 22 Reproduced by permission of the Christopher Ironside OBE estate; p. 25 Postal Museum; p. 26 Reproduced by permission of the Christopher Ironside OBE estate. A: 2006,0601.198, B: 2006,0601.197, C & D: 2006,0601.195; p. 27 Reproduced by permission of the Christopher Ironside OBE estate. 2006,0601.253, 2006,0601.255, 2006,0601.254, 2006,0601.251; p. 28 Reproduced by permission of the Christopher Ironside OBE estate. 2006,0601.250, 2006,0601.236, 2006,0601.244 and 2006,0601.246; p. 29 Reproduced by permission of the Christopher Ironside OBE estate. 2006,0601.165; p. 30 Reproduced by permission of the Christopher Ironside OBE estate. 2006,0601.158, 2006,0601.150; p. 31 Reproduced by permission of the Christopher Ironside OBE estate. 2006,0601.134; p. 32 Royal Mint Museum; p. 33 Royal Mint Museum; p. 34 Reproduced by permission of the Christopher Ironside OBE estate. Set 1: 2006,0601.431–436. Set 2: 2006,0601.437–443; p. 35 Reproduced by permission of the Christopher Ironside OBE estate. Set 3: 2006,0601.444–449. Set 4: 2006,0601.450–455; p. 36 Reproduced by permission of the Christopher Ironside OBE estate. 2006,0601.170; p. 37 Reproduced by permission of the Christopher Ironside OBE estate. 2006,0601.464Transport for London. British Museum Coins & Medals Archive; p. 38 Reproduced by permission of the Christopher Ironside OBE estate. 2006,0601.130, 2006,0601.140; p. 43 Reproduced by permission of the Christopher Ironside OBE estate. 2006,0601.143;p. 45 PA Images / Alamy Stock Photo. British Museum Coins & Medals Archive; p. 49 All rights reserved; p. 51 PA Images / Alamy Stock Photo. British Museum Coins & Medals Archive; p. 55 (Above) All rights reserved. British Museum Coins & Medals Archive. (Below) All rights reserved. British Museum Coins & Medals Archive; p. 56 All rights reserved. British Museum Coins & Medals Archive; p. 57 *New Money Dominoes*: All rights reserved. 2016,4058.1. *Snip Snap*: © Michael Stanfield / Ravensburger. 2016,4090.1. Mug: All rights reserved. British Museum Coins & Medals Archive; p. 58 (Above) All rights reserved. British Museum Coins & Medals Archive. (Right) All rights reserved. British Museum Coins & Medals Archive; p. 60 All rights reserved. British Museum Coins & Medals Archive; p. 62 2008,4113.6p; p. 64 2008,4113.6; All rights reserved. British Museum Coins & Medals Archive; p. 66 © The Sainsbury Archive, Museum of London Docklands; p. 68 Mirrorpix. British Museum Coins & Medals Archive; p. 69 (Above) Transport for London. British Museum Coins & Medals Archive. (Below) PA Images / Alamy Stock Photo. British Museum Coins & Medals Archive; p. 70 © Harrods Archive; p. 71 Photo: David Beer; p. 73 Michael Driver/Dinky Toy Collectors' Association; p. 78 Reproduced by permission of the Christopher Ironside OBE estate. 2006,0601.16.

The following objects have been licensed under the Open Government Licence v3.0. To view this licence, visit nationalarchives.gov.uk/doc/open-government-licence/

Opposite title page: 1969,1019.1; p. 7 1969,0903.30, 1978,0716.1 1968,0903.3; p. 15 copy of the Halsbury Report; p. 24 1969,1110.6; p. 40 1979,1125.9; p. 42 Bequeathed by Thomas Bryan Clarke-Thornhill. 1935,0401.8072; p. 44 2019,4122.1; p. 46 1978,0716.44, 1978,0716.37 (and back cover), 1978,0716.30; p. 47 1969,1110.5, 1969,1110.6, 1969,1019.1; p. 52 British Museum Coins & Medals Archive; p. 53 2019,4122.2; p. 59 Donated by Simmons and Simmons. 1969,0903.38; p. 76 2015,4018.2.